Cotton-Picking Folks

Eulogy for a Texas Depression Era Farm Family

Preston Lewis

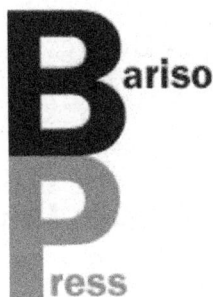

Bariso
Press

San Angelo, Texas

ISBN: 9798442540970
Imprint: Independently published

Cover design by: Preston Lewis
Edited by: Harriet Kocher Lewis

Library of Congress Control Number: 2022906170
Printed in the United States of America

**Dedicated to the Memory of
Carl Preston Lewis**

and his siblings

**Mildred McRorey
Marie Ammons
Myrt McRorey
Ella Mae Whitworth
Ray Franklin Lewis
John Bracken Lewis
Juanita Roberts**

Book One

West Texas Family Series

From Bariso Press

Table of Contents

CHAPTER ONE

Eulogy for a Texas Depression Era Farm Family

On a brisk December morning my brother and I buried John Bracken Lewis, our father, in Midway Cemetery just over a mile from the Jones County farm where he had built a house and lived more than four decades north of Abilene. Forty-one days later Juanita, his baby sister, died in Fort Worth, the last survivor of eight siblings from a bygone Texas era when cotton shaped families and destinies.

The eight—Mildred Ruth, Grace Marie, Edna Myrtle, Carl Preston, Ella Mae, Ray Franklin, John Bracken and Juanita Myrle—were born to Noah Preston and Ora Bell Lewis, my paternal grandparents, between 1912 and 1928. Born into a poverty that demanded their child labor, they all picked cotton before they could read and all faced a biscuit-and-gravy existence that typified the farm tenancy or crop lien system in Texas and the rest of the cotton South in the first five decades of the twentieth century. They matured as tenant farming reached its Texas zenith in a labor-intensive industry that sucked children into the state's cotton fields to feed the voracious global hunger for the versatile fiber.

"We started picking cotton early in life," Ella Mae recalled, "as that was one thing we could do, and every pound any of us picked just helped out that much."[1]

When John verged on his teen years, he told an adult neighbor, "I don't know what I'm going to be when I grow up, but one thing for sure I was not going to be a cotton farmer." Working cotton depleted the field hands just like it did the Texas soil.[2]

Cotton—like the families that produced it—is today

undervalued for its contribution to the state's economy and heritage, but for the first century of Texas as a colony, a nation and then a state, the fluffy commodity carried the economy bale by bale toward prosperity. While the word "Texas" may have meant "friendly" among early Indians, *The Texas Almanac and State Industrial Guide of 1926* noted, "in the world of commerce today it means 'cotton'."[3]

With their callused fingers, stooped backs and aching muscles, my kin contributed to that industry one cotton tuft after another, first in Collin and Dallas counties and then in the West Texas cotton fields of Nolan and Fisher counties, during the Depression and World War II. Though the industry they fed with their toil lacked the romance of the cattle trade and its iconic cowboys or the glamour of the rags-to-riches oil industry with its wanton wildcatters and gauche nouveau riche, cotton was the foundation fiber in the economic fabric of Texas from the beginning, a fact often overlooked by modern Texans largely because of its connections to slavery. The livestock trade spawned family empires like the Klebergs, the Waggoners, the Burnetts and the Schreiners, whose very names were synonymous with ranching. The oil business created great fortunes for families like the Cullens, the Basses, the Murchisons and the Hunts. The cotton industry produced thousands of anonymous families like my own that raised and harvested the crop but shared little in its ultimate wealth beyond a daily pittance.

Stephen F. Austin promoted cotton—not cattle and certainly not oil—for its agrarian viability and commercial profitability to convince the Mexican government to approve his original colony. Austin's first American colonists settled on the banks of the Brazos in 1821 and within a dozen years operated thirty cotton gins. By the time Texas cotton production was first recorded in 1849, farmers produced 58,073 bales of the fiber. While shipwreck survivor Cabeza de Vaca reported wild cotton growing in what became Texas as early as 1527, and while some Spanish missions around San Antonio grew cotton in the 1770s, Austin's colonists were the first to grow the fiber as a commercial crop. On the eve of the Civil War in 1860, Texas harvested 431,463 bales processed in almost 2,000 gins. Texas cotton continued to grow for decades, reaching a million bales in 1878, two million in 1891, three million in 1894 and four million in 1906. In 1926 Texas's 3,823 gins turned out 5.62 million bales, a record that stood for twenty-three years. The *1929 Texas Almanac and State Industrial Guide* estimated "70 percent of the population of the State is primarily dependent on cotton, directly or indirectly, for livelihood." By 1930 when the state's farm population peaked and all but sixteen of the state's 254 counties produced cotton, Lone Star farmers harvested 4.1 million bales processed at 3,651 active gins. For comparison, the state's 2020 upland cotton production came in at 4.7 million bales processed at 190 gins statewide.[4]

Austin's original colonists later came to be called the "Old Three Hundred," their descendants proudly claiming their lineage to those early Texans. My people, though lesser known today than even Austin's pioneers, were their economic if not blood descendants. None of my kin ever appeared by name in the history books, though my father, a then seventeen-year-old farm boy, rides anonymously through a handful of histories on women's aviation as a 1943 Texas cowboy aiding a downed Women Air Service Pilot from Sweetwater's Avenger Field. My folks never made the front page of the newspapers except for the worst possible reason, a tragic death in the family. Not one of the five sisters and three brothers spent a day in college, and only three left high school with diplomas. As tenant farm children, they grew up poor in material goods, scraping by through their sweat and toil in Texas's hot, dusty cotton fields, yet rich in a poverty-induced dedication to making better lives for themselves and their children.

Their class of humanity, though, was often scorned by contemporary intellectuals like Edward Everett Davis, dean from 1925 to 1946 of North Texas Agricultural College, forerunner of the University of Texas at Arlington. In the two-page introduction to his mediocre 1940 novel *The White Scourge,*[5] Davis called the cotton fields "the great open air slum of the South," noting that "too much of America's worthless silt has filtered into the cotton belt" where cotton culture provides a simple means of subsistence for "the South's rural proletariat composed of lowly blacks, peonized Mexicans and moronic whites numbering into several millions." Those were not just my people he was talking about, but thousands of other Texans as well. In 1930 when the crop lien system in Texas peaked, 301,660 of the state's 495,489 farms were harvested by farm tenants, sharecroppers and their families. By the time I finished Davis's introductory comments, I wondered if his novel's ambiguous title referred to the crop or to the morons that produced it. Ironically, the learned Davis dedicated his book to "The Cause of Rural Humanity."[6]

A more nuanced and sympathetic look at tenant farming appeared a year after Davis's book with George Sessions Perry's *Hold Autumn in Your Hand*, which traces a year in the life of a tenant farmer. Considered by some literary critics as the state's best agrarian novel, *Hold Autumn in Your Hand* in 1942 earned the National Book Award, the first ever presented to a Texas book, an irony for a state more associated in popular culture with the cowboy or the roughneck than the cotton farmer.[7]

Growing up in the 1950s, a decade when cowboys and westerns dominated the television airwaves, my brother Marc and I always played cowboys and Indians, never tenant farmers, as six-shooters and tomahawks offered greater recreational drama than the plows and hoes that dominated our family's cotton folklore. So, I never grasped the historical impact of cotton until I read Stephen Yafa's 2004 *Big Cotton: How A Humble Fiber Created Fortunes, Wrecked Civilizations, and Put America on the Map*. Cotton shaped our nation and the world more than the early livestock industry ever did. As Yafa noted, the fluffy fiber fed the Industrial Revolution in England; bled America during the Civil War; led the nation's first wave of American women into the workforce in New England's textile mills; and wed Marx and Engels to the ideas they promulgated in the *Communist Manifesto*. Beyond the denim jeans we wear today, cotton by-products, Yafa pointed out, are ubiquitous, whether in the books we read, the food we eat, the gum we chew, the coffee we filter or the paper money—which includes three quarters of a pound of cotton in each pound of currency printed by the U.S. Bureau of Engraving and Printing—we spend. "The source of cotton's

power," Yafa wrote, "is its nearly terrifying versatility and the durable creature comforts it provides."[8]

While my folks might have dreamed of creature comforts from the 1910s to the 1940s, survival remained the day-to-day reality of their hardscrabble lives as virtual serfs to the Texas cotton fields. "Cotton is, and has been throughout the history of the state, the chief dependence of the people of Texas," reported *The Texas Almanac and State Industrial Guide* of 1927. "The annual wealth produced from Texas cotton fields is practically equal, as an average, to the wealth production from all other crops of the State, from minerals including petroleum, from livestock and from forests."[9] My kin shared little in that wealth, but their stories of life as bit players in the cotton production chain during those decades enthralled me growing up as their recollections seemed—except for the automobile—so distant from my childhood that it was as if my dad, my aunts, and my uncles had come of age on the Texas frontier or even in Austin's Colony. So fascinated was I with their formative years that when I graduated from college in 1972, I suggested they record their "memoirs" of that era. Revisiting those handwritten and taped recollections after my father's and my last aunt's passing reminded me of the character and trials of that generation of Texans.

Of those years Dad regretted more than anything that his tenant farm mother, who died in 1942 when he was sixteen, never managed a household with running water and electricity, conveniences I took for granted as a child. I never knew my grandmother beyond a few photos and the stories her children told, but the contrast of two of her photographs haunts me. One was made about the time she graduated from Plano public schools in 1904. Taken either after her graduation or during her eight years teaching school before she

married, she is a young, slender woman with optimistic eyes, curly hair and a gentle, benign expression on her lips. The second shows her standing beside my grandfather in the early forties. Her slim figure has given way to middle-age girth; her hair is still short, but straight as if years of chores had wrung the curl from it; her lips bear a frown borne of too much work and too few rewards; and her empty eyes no longer reflect the optimism of youth, but rather the weariness of her arduous farm existence. The exhaustion in her face found words in a June 1941 letter she sent to two daughters: "I have been so busy this morning, have just found time to lay down and I am writing this laying down, hope you can read it."[10]

Rebecca Sharpless in *Fertile Ground, Narrow Choices*, a study of Texas cotton farm women from 1900 to 1940, described the farm tenancy female existence: "Rural women proved essential to their families' economic survival in ways that few middle-class urban women could match ... In this world of poverty and limited choices, bound by the movement of their husbands and the fortunes of the cotton crop, women worked to carve out their lives as best they could."[11]

Born in 1886, Ora Bell Garrett as a girl and young woman may never have considered life as a tenant farm matriarch because she earned a teacher's certificate the summer after graduating from high school in 1904 and taught in Collin County schools until 1911 when she at twenty-five married Noah Preston Lewis, who was just eighteen.[12] Born in 1893 N.P. or "Press," as he was called, was better suited to labor in the century of his birth than to the job market and economy that awaited him in the century of his maturity.[13] Early in their marriage he worked in a harness shop, then took up farming in

Collin and Dallas counties before moving to West Texas. Press migrated west like cotton, which had been confined to the eastern sections of Texas until the late 1880s. From the 1890s until 1910, cotton crept into the cattle country of middle West Texas in a band of neighboring counties extending from Hardeman to Runnels counties. From 1910-1930, cotton expanded into the South Plains and Panhandle as well as South Texas and the Lower Rio Grande Valley. Wherever cotton went grueling labor followed. All of N.P. Lewis's children agreed he was a hard worker without a lazy fiber in his lanky six-foot-two frame, but he lacked business skills or money-management sense.[14]

"Dad's family did not practice economy like Mother was taught to do," Mildred, the couple's oldest daughter, recalled, "so she was the one in our family who had to keep her foot on the brake, economy wise. A dollar to Dad was to spend and not to worry about whether or not he would need it worse for something more important the next day or month, but Mother looked ahead."[15]

The young Collin County couple first lived in Plano and Allen, then moved to Seagoville in southeast Dallas County where they welcomed three daughters: Mildred in 1912, Marie in 1913, and Myrtle, or "Myrt" as she was called, in 1915. A six-year childless gap followed before Carl Preston in 1921, Ella Mae in 1922 and Ray in 1923 were born in Seagoville. Ora always said she had three sets of children, the oldest girls, the Seagoville trio, and finally the youngest pair, John in 1926 and Juanita in 1928, both born on a farm near Roscoe in West Texas.[16] In those years a big family offered an edge to tenants renting farm acreage, as many landlords turned down potential renters because their offspring were too young or too few to work the fields.[17] From their move to West Texas until the children all left home—some voluntarily, some not—the vagaries of the cotton economy shaped their lives, their outlooks and, ultimately, their own children.

Unlike our father's generation, my brother and I never pulled a boll of cotton in our lives, but Dad's experience chopping and picking the plant fashioned our destiny as Dad instilled in us his work ethic, whether we wanted it or not. Living in the Permian

Basin a couple miles south of Midland, Dad made certain his two maturing sons handled plenty of chores—grubbing mesquites, chopping weeds, mowing the yard, painting our picket fence, shelling black-eyed peas, and anything else he thought needed done on our two-acre place. He paid us ten cents an hour for our time and labor. Hard as Marc and I believed our father drove us, it was play compared to what he and his siblings endured. They toiled in the field for survival. My brother and I just labored for money to buy baseball cards, comic books, bubble gum, and candy.

After Press's parents and a brother, one of his nine siblings, moved to Roscoe to farm in 1922, N.P. and his growing family visited them the next two summers, driving their old Model T to Nolan County, a two-day trip for them. They spent the night beside the road, and on one trip even had a car accident that bent an axle. They visited a blacksmith to get it straightened.[18]

Mildred remembered the second trip when she, Marie, Myrt and two of their cousins carried homemade wooden paddles to the field where giant grasshoppers emerged from the pasture along the fence rows to devour the cotton plants. The children swatted hundreds of grasshoppers to save the crop. Grasshoppers or not, in the fall of 1924 Press moved Ora and their six children, ranging from one to twelve years old, from the blackland soil of Dallas County to the red sandy loam of Nolan County, originally settled in the late 1870s and organized in 1881. The county straddled the divide between the Brazos watershed to the north and the Colorado watershed to the south. Primarily ranching country in its early years, the county slowly moved to farming after the turn of the century with 33,000 acres planted in cotton in 1910, increasing to 80,000 acres by 1930. In the decade between 1920 and 1930, farms increased from 1,015 to 1,514, a 49 percent hike, and the population grew from 10,868 to 19,323, a 78 percent increase.[19] In relocating to Nolan County with so many others, Press ignored the unpredictability and overall scarcity of West Texas rainfall—about twelve inches less a year than in North Texas—and the destructiveness of West Texas windstorms. He and a neighbor who was also moving to Roscoe jointly rented a railroad freight car to transport their belongings to

Nolan County. There, the Lewis family first shared a four-room house with Press's brother Clint, who they helped gather his 1924 crop.[20]

That year, 9.44 million acres, or 56.7 percent of Texas's 16.65 million cropland acres, grew cotton. Texas farmers and their 3,652 gins produced more than 25 percent of the *world's* cotton in 1924. Five years later just as the Stock Market crashed, one economist estimated that a third of the state's population farmed cotton. Thousands more Texans worked downwind from the cotton farmer in transporting and warehousing, compressing and marketing, merchandising and cottonseed processing. In those years Galveston reigned as the nation's largest cotton port.[21]

On New Year's Day 1925, Press took possession of a farm north of Roscoe near Wastella, thus beginning the nomadic life of a West Texas tenant farmer. The next year, when the Lewises moved to the Val Forrester place, southwest of Roscoe where Dad and Juanita were born, Texas cotton acreage peaked at 17.74 million acres. By contrast Texas cotton farmers in 2020 planted only 6.8 million acres of the fiber.[22]

During his four-year tenure on the Forrester property, Press "farmed on the halves" as a sharecropper, earning half of the harvest from the landowner for his family's toil. Once he bought his own farm animals and equipment, he transferred his family to the nearby Younger place in 1930 for a year as a tenant farmer with more control and a greater percentage of his harvest. The next year they relocated to the Woodard place northwest of Roscoe through the 1932 harvest, the family's best. A disagreement between N.P. and the property owner over the lease-length went to court before the family was evicted. Forced to rent new farmland, Press found the Copeland place west of Blackwell in southern Nolan County, where the family labored through the 1933 and 1934 harvests. Then Press took his family north to the Busby community in Fisher County where he farmed through 1943 on the C.H. Bolin place.[23] That tumbleweed lifestyle typified a tenant farmer's existence, the poorer the farmer, the more frequent the moves. Texas tenant farmers averaged a move every 3.5 years, sharecroppers every 2.3 years.[24]

The N.P. Lewis family's nine-year tenure on the Bolin place was their longest and final lease of a tenant farm. They lived near the unincorporated community of Busby, about ten miles south of Roby, the seat of Fisher County, which was organized in 1886. In Busby the five youngest children matured, going to the Busby school before attending high school in either Roby or Sweetwater. Like Nolan County, its neighbor to the south, Fisher County started in the 1870s as sparsely settled ranchlands that eventually transitioned to farm properties. The rolling prairie lands of sandy loam soil drained to the Double Mountain Fork and the Clear Fork of the Brazos River and produced wheat, corn, oats and cotton, of course. In 1928, the year the value of petroleum in Texas first exceeded the value of cotton, oil was discovered in Fisher County, helping some landowners survive the economic downturn ahead and the regulatory effects of government agricultural policy during the Great Depression. By 1930 64 percent of Fisher County's 2,088 farmers worked someone else's land. The Fisher County population during the Great Depression dropped from 13,563 in 1930 to 12,932 in 1940.[25]

Throughout his farming career from World War I through World War II, my grandfather never held title to the land he worked. I once made the mistake of calling him a sharecropper, but Dad quickly corrected me. N.P. Lewis was a tenant farmer—at least after leaving the Forrester place—because he provided his own mules, farm implements, seed, and labor while sharecroppers just offered their toil. As a tenant farmer, Press owned the crop, allowing him to mortgage it with the bank, and paid the landowner with a third of his grain and a fourth of his cotton harvest. By contrast a sharecropper held no claim to the crop, the landlord owning it and typically paying half the harvest to the sharecropper for his family's labor.[26] The 1930 census determined nearly a quarter of *all* Texans lived under the crop lien system, accounting for more than 60 percent of the state's farmers—the highest percentage ever—as the Great Depression set in. The Civil War may have ended bondage, but King Cotton did not on the state's 495,489 farms because of the labor-intensive hand-harvesting that had changed little since the first historical records of cotton centuries before the common era.[27]

Whether tenant farmers or sharecroppers, the entire family labored hard to survive on the farm, the children starting chores at an early age. Mildred, for instance, learned to milk a cow so young that she never recalled receiving any instruction. "I was nine years old ... when I learned to make biscuits and had to help with the family meals from there on," she noted. The oldest daughter assisted her mother with the cooking, with raising her siblings, and with clothing the family. "We did not know what it was like to have many store-bought ones (clothes) so we provided our own," Mildred remembered. Once Ora taught her to operate their treadle sewing machine, Mildred made drawers and dresses for her siblings from feed and flour sacks. And, Mildred worked in the fields with her father like all his children as they grew up. Her younger sister Myrt recalled, "I was young, but I remember the work I had to help do: pick cotton, shuck corn, feed the pigs and horses, carry in wood winter and summer for we cooked on a wood stove, dozens of evening chores that modern kids know nothing about. But it wasn't all bad, to sit in the trough and eat peanuts with the horses was fun, if you didn't eat too many. I made a game out of pumping water with the pitcher pump, jumping every time I pumped. Cows to milk morning and night, but that cream was delish on Post Toasties."[28]

The three oldest daughters had the roughest go of Press's offspring because they carried a heavy load in the field as well as in the house. Mildred remembered one year of harvesting cotton "on top of all the days and days of canning peas, beans, corn, okra, pumpkin, and pickles, but there was very little money so that is mostly what we lived on the next year."[29]

When Press began farming the Forrester place in 1926, cotton was selling at 12.47 cents a pound, rising to 20.19 cents the following year. Average cotton prices would not surpass the 1927 level again until 1944, the year Press quit farming. Prices dropped from 1927 to 1931 when they bottomed out at 5.66 cents per pound, forcing Press to take a job at the U.S. Gypsum plant in Sweetwater one year, leaving it to his three oldest daughters to put in the cotton.[30]

"Marie, Myrt, and I made the crop," Mildred said. "Dad had

three teams and three one-row plows, planters, so we each had our own team. That was quite an experience, but we got the job done and even learned to set our own plows." Mildred worked her team so much that year that it affected her driving. When she got permission to take the car and her sisters to Roscoe, both Marie and Myrt giggled every time she approached a stop sign and called "whoa." As Marie explained, "She had plowed more than she had driven."[31]

Such humor eased the stress of Depression-era realities. According to Marie, "Mother and Daddy had a way of discussing the family finances at the table and *[that]* made us feel we had a part in it. We were always concerned when our prospects for a crop were not good. In fact, I can't remember many times *[of]* we older girls asking for money, for we usually knew Daddy didn't have it to spare." Myrt recalled, "Our daddy worked hard, and so did the rest of the family, but when half of it *[the crop]* belonged to the landowner, a living was all we had. I don't ever remember going hungry, but many times our evening meal was hot biscuits, cream gravy, butter, and syrup."[32]

The properties Press rented came with a dwelling, usually a clapboard house, often with a roof that dripped water during occasional but drenching showers. Drafty walls admitted dust when the wind blew and screen-less doors and windows let in flies all the time. "I can remember," John said, "Mother and the older girls taking towels, opening the back door and starting at the front and waving the towels to drive the flies out the back door." And the structures were small. Myrt described their first West Texas family home. "We lived in a two-room house, one bedroom with three big beds in it. Different times in rent houses our family was so crowded for bedrooms, sometimes six to the room. Modern families probably think it couldn't be done, but we did it, and it didn't hurt us. Also, our bathrooms were non-existent. Those old rent houses just didn't have bathrooms just a path to an outhouse with a sagging door and highly infested with all kinds of crawling things."[33]

During their two years on the Copeland place near Blackwell, all ten of the Lewis family shared a four-room house. Besides the kitchen, the front room doubled as the parlor and bedroom for

Press and Ora; the two oldest daughters shared a second bedroom; and a back room held two double beds less than a foot apart where the six remaining siblings slept, three brothers in one bed and three sisters in the other.[34]

Just like adequate shelter, food—or the lack of it—remained a daily challenge. Sure, they gardened, but every square foot of land they devoted to vegetables and their sustenance subtracted from the acreage available for cotton and grain sorghum, their money crops, sometimes to the dismay of landowners under pressure to meet their mortgages.[35] Ora and Press bought their staples at the store, but raised chickens for eggs, fed cows for milk, and gardened each summer for vegetables, including black-eyed peas, yellow squash, green beans, and cucumbers. In season, Ora added the vegetables to the family's table fare and canned what she could in Mason jars for the cold, barren winter months ahead.[36]

"Dad always had some meat hogs to butcher in the fall of each year and, oh my, what a delight when it came time to do that," Mildred said. "Our first meal from the hogs was fried liver, milk gravy with hot biscuits, and the traditional sorghum syrup. As soon as Dad gutted the hogs, he would cut out the melts (spleen) and give them to us kids to roast on the fire around the old wash pots where they heated the water to scald the hogs in order to remove the hair … Then, of course, there was the sausage to grind and [stuff] in [casings] made from flour sacks. It was not an easy job to put all that meat through the old sausage mill either, but a cake of sausage in a biscuit made the best sandwich ever in our school lunches … Then the fat from the hogs had to be rendered into lard out in the old wash pots and stored away in five- and ten-gallon lard stands. The cracklin's were then used to make lye soap to do the family laundry; also we used it to shampoo our hair, for we simply did not have anything else. When the hams, shoulders and sides of bacon were all cured out, they were sacked and hung from the rafters of the smokehouse. This meat would last for quite a while, but not quite all year." Farm families joked they used all the hog but the squeal.[37]

Press always gave the hog bladders to his kids as a treat. "We would get a hollow straw and blow those stinking things up for balloons and balls," Mildred said. "They really made good volleyballs and would last a long time and get blacker and blacker as they collected more and more dirt, but we had fun playing with them."[38]

"Toys were nonexistent," youngest son John recalled. "If we had anything to play with, we had to make it." As a youngster John would use empty bottles for horses and build little plows from twigs for amusement. "Mother had a potato masher, a hand potato masher, which she would let me play with some because it made a good harrow in the sand." He would take a block of wood, some nails, and the lids from baking soda cans for wheels to build a car. Childhood necessity made John a junkyard engineer for life. As an adult he would resurrect discarded or worn-out goods, like making a barbecue pit out of a 55-gallon drum or using duct tape to repair his worn canvas sneakers so they would last a little longer. As a young father, he engineered my brother and me a go-cart, built us a backstop to play baseball, and even bought us a donkey for a steed in our young cowboy fantasies. He said his dearth of toys as a boy inspired him to provide those for his sons. Likewise, when it came to our dinner table, he insisted Mom prepare large meals with bread, potatoes, vegetables, meat and dessert because he didn't want his boys to ever worry about their next meal.[39]

As for the girls' amusement, they often found their entertainment in the cottonseed bin. Press saved cottonseed for the next year's crop and to feed the milk cows because Ora thought cottonseed made the cows give better milk, spawning a prettier yellow butter. "The seed house was our favorite place to play," Mildred recalled. "We built all kinds of castles and cities in the cottonseed." Her baby sister Juanita also loved the seed house. "I used to have fun playing in the cottonseed bin, piling cottonseed up higher and jumping off into it. I had to entertain myself, since we had no close neighbors to come to play or to go visit." Ella Mae remembered visiting one distant neighbor's house and finding a virtually new catalog in the outhouse. "Oh, it had some of the best-looking paper dolls. I wanted that catalog so bad that ... I raked up the courage to ask her. She was so gracious to give it to me and ... Mother let me sit up later than usual that night and burn some of the kerosene oil in our lamp that we had to be so saving with to cut out paper dolls. I had boy dolls, girl dolls, and baby dolls. I would spend hours playing with them."[40]

Play also presented country hazards, especially for the brothers. Over the years Ray recovered from a kick in the stomach by a mare named "Shine." Carl Preston stepped on a pincushion cactus that required his three older sisters to hold him down while his father cut the thorns out with a knife. John tripped on a piece of bailing wire that pierced through the top of his foot. Press used kerosene to sterilize both boys' feet after the primitive surgeries. John also broke his arm attempting to swing on a rope across the creek and got sprayed in the face by a skunk while trying to flush it from a bush so his brother Ray could shoot him with a slingshot.[41]

Beyond the boyhood injuries, the three sons learned to hunt and used a single-shot .22-caliber rifle to augment their diet with cotton tails, squirrels, turtles and even bullfrogs for their meaty legs. When they lived near creeks, the boys caught fish. Their sisters learned to hunt and fish as well, most enjoying those outdoor skills along with their brothers well past their retirements. Besides providing food for the table, hunting and fishing offered a respite from the tedium of cotton farming, though not without its hazards. Ella Mae remembered her father going creek fishing with his brothers once. "Dad lost his billfold and all the money we had was in there," she recalled. "He had to borrow enough money to get us by until the first bale of cotton *[came in]*. I just can't imagine now not having one penny and a family of ten, but that was the way we lived back then."[42]

Like fishing, raising cotton could be a money-losing proposition, an annual gamble akin to turn-row roulette with potential losses from insects—boll weevils, bollworms, flea hoppers, leafworms, cutworms, stalk borers, cotton strainers, leaf beetles and red spiders—and disease, primarily cotton blight as well as root knot, boll rot, rust, soreskin and bacterial blight. The unpredictability of both market prices and the weather added to the tenant farmer's gambles. Plentiful rains at the right time were a blessing, but the same rain at the wrong time could wash away newly planted fields in the spring or stunt the crop's maturity late in the summer when hot, dry skies were needed for optimum growth and maturity. Hailstorms or damaging winds could wipe out a crop. "We kids always enjoyed the walk after a rain to look over the crop," Ella Mae recalled. "Usually, Dad, Mother, and the young ones who could walk would go." John remembered dinner table conversations between his parents. "If they made enough money to pay off all their debts or he could borrow enough money to make the next crop on, they felt like they had had a pretty good year."[43]

Oldest daughter Mildred recalled the 1932 crop on the Woodard place northwest of Roscoe producing a great harvest because of decent rains and seasonable weather. The family that year gathered seventy-six bales, which based on the year's average price earned them 6.52 cents per pound, barely a penny more than the all-time low of 1931. "Dad made such a good crop of everything, but things were so cheap that it didn't amount to very much." At 500 pounds per bale, Press grossed, not counting indeterminable ginning fees, $2,478 on cotton, netting $1,858 after paying the landlord his fourth. The family that year also harvested a hundred tons of grain sorghum, which they sold in town for four dollars a ton, netting another $267 after paying the landlord his third share. A year of hard field work in 1932 earned $2,125, the equivalent of $41,422 in today's dollars for a family of ten. The 2021 Federal Poverty Level for a family of 10 totaled $53,740. My folks were poor, even by contemporary standards.[44]

Press may have received some income from his cottonseed, which by 1932 had become a major commodity thanks to chemical processes that rendered seeds into oil, cake or meal, hulls, and linters, the cellulose rich fiber stubs left on the seed after ginning. Cottonseed oil was used in margarine, salad oil and shortening; meal/cake for fertilizer and livestock feed; hulls for the furfural essential for manufacturing synthetic rubber during the war; and linters to produce smokeless gunpowder. In fact when the Federal government during the war increased allowable cotton acreages, it was because the government needed the cottonseed products more than the fiber. The volume of raw cotton that produced a 500-pound bale of fiber also turned out a thousand pounds of cottonseed. During the 1920s and 1930s,

cottonseed usually ranked as the state's third most valuable agricultural commodity, occasionally surpassing corn for second place on the value rankings.[45]

In addition to feeding his livestock cottonseed, N.P. also raised grain sorghum for the same purpose, always selling his surplus. Like cotton, the grain was harvested by hand. Since sorghum grew atop a stalk, it required less stoop work than picking cotton. Field hands walked down the rows with a harvesting tool much like a curved utility knife and cut the stalk just beneath the head. "We'd take a knife and a sled and go to the field with a horse hooked to this sled," John recalled. "The old horses were trained where you could tell them to 'get up' and they would walk up two or three steps while you headed up three or four feet and threw the maize in this box *[on the sled]*. When you got up to this box, you would tell the horse to 'get up' a little bit farther, and that is the way the maize was gathered." When the box filled, the gatherers dumped it on the ground to dry before being stored or sold.[46]

Despite the chores involved in heading sorghum, it was always cotton that shaped the bittersweet memories of their early years, as that crop influenced the clothes they wore and the very education they received. John recalled, "I had to wear overalls and blue denim shirts to school. I sure did want to wear trousers or what we called 'waistbands,' but Mother and Dad seemed to think that overalls were much more practical because you could work in them whenever they got a bit ragged or too ragged to wear to school. I was probably in the eighth grade before I was allowed to wear anything but overalls to school." As Myrt remembered, "Our clothes were few, too: Two new school dresses for a season and a pair of shoes, which I always had trouble making mine last." The irony of their meager wardrobe was that the cotton they and their Texas predecessors picked between 1850 and 1936, some 180 million-plus bales, is estimated to have "clothed probably 15 or 20 percent of the civilized people of the world."[47]

Cotton not only influenced their school clothes but also the academic calendar. "We wouldn't get to start school when it started because we'd have to pick cotton," John said. "I remember a lot of times staying out of school for as high as six or eight weeks to pick cotton. In fact, sometimes there were enough kids out of school picking cotton that they would just turn school out right there in the main part of the cotton-picking season." The *1928 Texas Almanac* noted, that beyond the agricultural challenges of farm tenancy, "it is largely in the tenant element that the problems of rural education, child labor and rural sanitation are encountered."[48]

The cotton cycle began in late April or early May, with the planting of seeds three or four inches apart. Once the seeds sprouted and the shoots pushed through the soil, the plants had to be thinned or "chopped," as it was called. Chopping aimed to leave a stalk every eight to ten inches, so each remaining plant had space to grow and mature without crowding and stunting its neighbors. The task also allowed the farmer to sacrifice thin, pale yellow cotton sprouts in favor of stockier, more productive dark green plants.[49] Press, his sons and his daughters all chopped cotton by the time they began first grade. Family members would start in the mornings at the end of a row and begin the tedious hoeing. An experienced chopper, Press worked fast and far ahead of his children, often stepping to one of his offspring's rows and thinning their plants before resuming work on his own row. "Daddy was a good teacher and very patient with us," Marie remembered. "He could chop the neatest, most uniform row of cotton I ever saw and tried to teach us the same. It was great to come to a nice long 'skip' that Daddy had hoed to help us *[keep]* up with him. That 'skip' just seemed to say, 'I love you, come on up'."[50]

Once the cotton had been thinned, it matured, blooming in June and the ensuing cotton bolls bloating into August when, swollen with fiber, they burst open and the casings, or burrs, began to dry, harden and blacken as the white cotton tuft emerged. Throughout the growing months the family hoed weeds to keep them from dwarfing the cotton and stealing valuable moisture and nutrients from the soil. Then in late September or early October, when the bolls had dried, the family started picking the seed cotton by hand.[51] The stoop work was hot, dusty and repetitive, leaving fingers scratched and cracked from the prickly burrs and stiff from the repetitive motion. Adult pickers could choose between back pain if they stooped to harvest or knee pain if they knelt. Rather than bend over all day, the lanky Press wore homemade kneepads and gathered cotton on his knees, as if he were perpetually praying for a good yield.[52]

Before gins became sophisticated enough to separate the burrs from the cotton, pickers extracted the fiber from the dried hulls and shoved the cotton tufts in twelve-foot-long canvas sacks that they dragged down the rows. As cotton gin technology improved, field hands could pull the entire boll, but for most years N.P. farmed his family extracted the fiber from the burs rather than pulling it from the stalk. It could take as many as two hundred bolls to produce a single pound of seed cotton with the lint still attached to the seed. An experienced picker could gather 150 to 300 pounds of seed cotton a day, while a highly skilled laborer might collect up to 500 pounds daily.[53]

When their bags filled, family members carried them to a high-sided wagon where the accumulation was weighed and then dumped in the back. Once the wagon filled with the 1,500 to 1,600 pounds it required to make a 500-pound bale, Press would hitch up the team and pull it to the gin, where the seed cotton was again weighed and sampled to determine the grade, which set the price.[54]

Press always insisted that his children start young and pick cotton by age. John first remembered harvesting the fiber on the Woodard place, which meant he was six years old when he began in the fields. At the end of the workday, Press believed the older children should have tallied a greater weight in their sack than their younger siblings. Oldest daughter Mildred proved the exception. "I was always called the old cow's tail of the family for being so slow, but Dad impressed on me so much that anything worth doing was worth doing right, and if I only hoed or picked one row of cotton a day to do it right, so I really tried to do just that. The rest of the family sure did hate to help me out when quitting time came, but they would rather *[do that]* than leave me out there all alone to finish my row. However, Dad always put my cotton on the front of the wagon because it was clean and free of trash, and they always took the sample off the front of the wagon at the gin, so maybe my slowness paid off a little."[55]

"Our first cotton sack was made out of a forty-pound flour sack," Ella Mae said. "Then as we grew, we used a tow sack. Then Mother would take the good part of Dad's and the older girls' worn-out sacks and make us one. Then came the year I got my first brand new one. Oh, how proud I was of that new sack! The first day I used it, I remember so well trying to see how much it would hold. So, I would sit down on the ground and put my feet in the sack and pack it just as much as possible. When *[we]* weighed *[it]*, there was forty pounds in there. Boy, did I feel like I had really done something."[56]

One fall day in the Bolin cotton field, Ray and Ella Mae had goofed off much of the afternoon as she recounted. An hour before quitting time, Press pointed out that their little brother was picking cotton as fast as he could. Press warned Ray and Ella Mae that when quitting time came, they would get a whipping if their sacks weighed out less than his. Both increased their pace, Ella Mae bawling and Ray grumbling at their little brother's treachery. Come quitting time, Ella Mae had out-picked John by a pound and Ray by a half-pound, much to the disappointment of their younger brother. Such mischief provided memorable moments from an otherwise monotonous task.[57]

Since cotton bolls opened at sporadic times, the field had to be picked multiple times. "We would have to pull over the same field two or three times and sometimes four," Ella Mae remembered. "When we would move from one field to another, how we would wish we were through instead of moving to another field."[58]

In a letter posted November 1, 1935, to her oldest sister, Ella Mae wrote, "Just guess how much we all got today? 1,208 *[pounds]*. Pretty good for what we had been getting, around 600." She bragged of harvesting 200 pounds on her own for the day. Ella Mae was thirteen years old. John, in a separate note to Mildred that same day, reported picking 157 pounds. He was just nine. In an accompanying letter, Ora explained the reason for the day's big haul by "Papa," as she called Press, and her five children still at home. "Carl plowed in wheat up until Tues. eve.

then went to picking cotton. They did the biggest day's picking today they've done this year, 1208 lbs. I believe they said Papa and Carl ran a race, and son beat him by a few lbs. Papa was almost played out when they quit."[59]

After all the cotton had been gathered and ginned, sometimes as late as January, Press then had to shred the stalks, spread manure saved from the farm animals, and plow the field to repeat the cycle of planting, chopping, weeding, picking, ginning and selling the crop.

In addition to cotton, romance also bloomed in the fields where the Copeland cropland abutted the McRorey place outside Blackwell, where Myrt met Bill McRorey, her future husband. "Our courtship was mostly in the cotton patch," she remembered. "The families worked together a lot. Bill and I would take rows together and would get ahead of the rest. How is that for a romantic courtship? ... Our folks were all picking cotton the day we married. We quit from Wednesday for the rest of the week. We went to Roscoe and the old Baptist preacher Rev. G.W. Parks married us in his home. He had to go spit out his snuff. He said his wife was upstairs quilting, but he didn't bother to call her, so we had no witnesses, just Bill and me and the preacher. We went to Grandpa and Grandma Lewis's for dinner."[60]

Myrt's oldest sister Mildred would later marry Bill's brother Arnold, and both couples would live out their lives in Blackwell. Myrt would bear three of Press's and Ora's fourteen grandchildren. Mildred and Arnold, however, never had children. I asked Mildred one time why she had passed on having kids. "By the time I left home," she replied, "I had already raised one family." Cotton farming took its toll on everyone.

All the hardships they endured in the field and at the dinner table strengthened the bonds of family. That was why losing oldest son Carl Preston Lewis devastated the close-knit clan in 1937.

Born August 4, 1921, Carl Preston was the first boy in the family and a farmhand in the making. "We were all so proud of our little brother, and naturally Dad was elated over his first son," Mildred said. Just as I never knew my grandmother, I never met Carl Preston, though he is with me daily in the name I carry. I learned of him through the family tales and the surviving photos. He always looks so young and vigorous with an impish grin. My favorite photo is of him on the front porch of their Busby home with his parents, Ella Mae, Juanita and his two brothers, both in overalls, while Carl Preston wore waistbands, a shirt and a flat cap at a rakish tilt. It shows a happy family unaware of impending tragedy just months away.[61]

In November 1937 Carl Preston traveled with his Roby High teammates to Colorado City for the last football game of the season. He scored on a 50-yard fumble recovery that would be the difference in the Lions' 13-7 upset of the Wolves, but as he made a diving tackle on a subsequent play, his leg struck another player's

Clockwise from top left, N.P., Ella Mae, Ora, Carl, Ray, John and Juanita, 1937

thigh, breaking his fibula. He managed one more down before realizing he was injured and hobbling off the field. Back home he visited a Sweetwater doctor, who told him and his parents he could avoid surgery, but would likely limp the rest of his life. Press left the decision to Carl, who opted to undergo the operation. After being anesthetized with ether, Carl Preston aspirated, the resulting infection weakening his lungs and leading to the pneumonia that killed him early Thanksgiving morning

1937. That afternoon's *Sweetwater Reporter* ran a banner headline TRAGEDIES MAR THANKSGIVING DAY IN SWEETWATER with a subhead ROBY GRIDIRON STAR DIES OF PNEUMONIA. The next day's *Abilene Reporter-News* announced his passing on the front page: ROBY FOOTBALL PLAYER IS DEAD.[62]

"The sad thing that I remember was the night he died," John recalled. "Dad and Marie came home and told Mother and the other girls that Carl had died, and we heard Mother and the other sisters crying and screaming. It was so sad."[63]

"Mother," Mildred said, "was never well any more after this. She lived five years after we lost Carl, but she would have a real bad sick spell every year about October and November. I always thought Mother bottled up her grief over the loss of Carl, trying to make it easier for the rest of us."[64]

In his billfold at his death, Carl Preston carried two photos of Inell Edwards, who would likely have become my aunt had Carl Preston lived. She sat with the family during the funeral services, holding John's hand and comforting him as he took the loss the hardest. More than a half century later, Dad drove me by the building, now a pharmacy, that was Sweetwater Hospital in 1937. Dad pointed to a window and told me that was the room where his brother had died. He broke down at the recollection and could not say another word for several minutes. After the war when he and his surviving brother had their first children, each a boy, Ray named his son Carl and Dad named me Preston.[65]

"This was such a trying time for the family to lose someone so young and full of life and health and also our first real tragedy in the family," Mildred said. "I don't think we were really prepared to accept it, at least I know I wasn't at that time *[because]* it looked so useless to me."[66]

In writing her recollections of growing up, Myrt briefly mentioned the death of Carl Preston and other family members later. "I have not told about so many of our sad times, but we had them ... Yes, many tears have been mingled with our joys, but someone has said that if the eyes had no tears, the soul would have no rainbow. So through it we have clung to the Old Rugged Cross and the One who is able to sustain us in all things."[67]

In listening to their recollections of life on a West Texas cotton farm, I came to believe that faith, music, and humor sustained them through such difficult times.

Ora was a member of the First Christian Church in Collin County, while she married into a family from the Baptist tradition, creating some tensions from the demeaning comments her father-in-law made about her religion. Mildred said Ora was a religious role model. "She was the most understanding Christian, and so broad minded about everything." When thunderstorms would frighten her offspring, Mildred recalled "Mother used to tell us a story about how the splattering raindrops were little people on their way to church. She had a very special way of making us feel safe."[68]

Mildred remembered how various churches they attended "would have all-day services sometimes, and everyone would bring their dinner and spread it on long lines of white tablecloths on the ground under some huge trees. That was always a great day for me. Baptism services were always held at a big tank of water in a big pasture." For instance, my father John joined the Liberty Baptist Church in Busby a little over a year after his brother's death and was baptized in a stock tank on a nearby farm. All the siblings save Carl Preston were baptized, a fact that tormented the family throughout their lives.[69]

Mildred finally came to terms with her oldest brother's death almost a decade later after Ray returned safely home from fighting in Europe. "The Lord blessed us again in keeping Ray safe ... [It was] after he got home from the war that I finally got my answer as to why Carl was taken like he was, for I came to realize all of a sudden just how much he and all of us may have been spared, and I was able at last to thank God for it." Yes, they had buried a son and brother, but they had at least been able to provide him a Christian burial in his native soil, unlike the parents and siblings of so many war dead in the European and Pacific theaters.[70]

Music helped them get through Carl Preston's loss as well as the difficult times as a tenant farm family. Prior to his death, the family installed a wind charger atop the house that charged batteries enough that they could listen to the radio, but before that and afterward as well, they sang and played music. Carl Preston played a harmonica; Myrt a guitar; and Ella Mae and ultimately Juanita a piano. Somehow during those lean Depression years in Busby, Press and Ora acquired a piano, then used egg and butter money to hire a teacher to give rudimentary lessons to Ella Mae. With limited instruction from Ella Mae, Juanita relied on her musical ear to later master the talent. Juanita remembered, "I used to sit at the window sill and pretend to play with the music on the radio, or just sing a song and play like I was playing the piano."[71]

Mildred said, "Our family sang a lot together. Dad played the French-harp and picked the guitar. He fixed some kind of wire rack that fit around his neck to hold the *[harmonica]* so he could play it and pick the guitar at the same time. Mother had a beautiful voice; also Marie had such a nice soprano voice. I tried my luck with alto, as that seemed to fit my range best. Myrt had the widest range of all as she could manage tenor, alto, or soprano. We all loved those family singing sessions ... After we older girls married and would gather home for visits ... we would all gather around the piano for a sing-song, religious, popular, and some ballads, with Juanita and Ella Mae at the piano ... We had fun."[72]

As I grew up around my dad's brother and sisters during visits and the annual family reunions, I remember laughter more than music or anything else. The brothers and sisters relished telling stories about the pranks the brothers pulled or the funny incidents that occurred growing up in dire circumstances. In their later years humor seemed to lessen their childhood hardships, but I never knew for certain if that was the tenor of their Depression-era existence or merely the sheen on their memories as they recalled their hardscrabble youths.

"We were poor," Ella Mae told me one time, "but we just didn't know it because everybody else was pretty much in the same shape, so we pretty much had to laugh at things." Mildred echoed those sentiments. "Most everyone else was in the same financial bind, so we could all laugh about it and share what we did have. In fact, I truly believe everyone was happier then than they are now with all their material gain."[73]

The boys' mischief usually topped the humorous stories. Ella Mae recalled an afternoon picking cotton when Press sent Ray back to the house to re-fill the water jug. She asked Ray to bring back the wad of chewing gum she had stuck under the table at lunch. Ray obliged, but only after punching a hole in it, filling the cavity with pepper and molding the wad around the surprise spice. Ella Mae choked when she bit into her wad, but chewing gum was too precious to spit out, so she kept chomping it until the bitter taste dissipated days later. She despised pepper for the rest of her life. Ray recalled how he and his brothers loved to tip over the sled boxes when their sisters were heading maize, no matter if it meant extra work for everyone.[74]

John and Ray both remembered building what today would be called a zip line at Busby. They slid a length of pipe over a makeshift cable they had made from all the old wire they could find around the place and secured the line to a tree on one end and a post on the other. "We were a little bit afraid to try it ourselves," John said, "so we hit on the bright idea of talking Eller into climbing up in this tree and riding this trolley down under the pretense that we were just going to let her be first. What we really wanted to know was if the wire was strong enough to hold *us*." Ella Mae, the most gullible of the siblings, climbed the tree, slid about four feet down the improvised line, then tumbled eight or ten feet to the ground when the cable broke. When she landed on her back, the impact knocked the breath out of her. John remembered her crying, "I can't talk. I can't talk" instead of yelling that she couldn't breathe. At the same time, she threatened to go to the house and tell of their mischief. "We finally got her breathing back, made a few promises and talked her out of going to tell on us ... and that was the way it all wound up," he said.[75]

Nothing, though, brought more laughter than flatulence. Farts seemed to prove God had a sense of humor when he created man and woman. Ray recalled an old mule named Tobe that would break wind whenever they goosed him with a stick. The boys loved to poke him whenever their sisters were around. Mildred recalled a Sunday church service when either Myrt or a boy cousin her age broke wind. "They got so tickled that Mother and Aunt Ione like never to have got them to hush and were so embarrassed by their children's behavior," she recounted, then reconsidered. "Actually, I think they were as tickled as the kids were." Then there were Ella Mae's mental lapses, what would today be called "brain farts," like the time Carl Preston came home from school embarrassed after a lesson on the fall of the Alamo when Ella Mae piped up to her classmates, "Did it really fall down?"[76]

Ella Mae was no scholar, but a tomboy and a tremendous athlete. "I was born in between the three brothers, and it seemed they delighted in aggravating me," she said. "Because of this, I learned to take care of myself early in life. I could outrun any of them, and *[I]* give them credit for being pretty good athletes." At Blackwell school a male classmate had boasted of winning an interscholastic league race the previous weekend when Ella Mae overheard him. "He was kind of bragging about how good he was, so showoff me challenged him for a race," Ella Mae said, "and I won. Poor boy wouldn't even come back to where the other kids were watching and laughing. I sure felt like I had really done something." She beat him so badly that he never stopped, just kept running home and didn't return to school until the next day. Ella Mae became such a family athletic legend that years later I, acknowledged by all as the slowest afoot of my generation, challenged her to a footrace and actually won. I was in my early thirties when she was in her mid-sixties, but Eller was always game—and gullible—for anything.[77]

As the children aged, their humorous stories got more mature, like the time Ray went from Busby to visit his city cousin Bub in Sweetwater. There Ray got his first lesson in how to pick up girls. "Bub was gonna show his country cousin how it was done," Ray remembered, so he pulled over and stopped his Model T by two cute young ladies walking down the sidewalk. "He said, 'Hi, girls, how about going for a ride with us?' And one of them said, 'You got any gas?' And he said, 'Yeah, I got a tank full.' They said, 'Well, crank up and go to hell then!' … That was the last lesson I got from Bub on how to pick up girls."[78]

Their faith, their music and their humor got them through their hard times, but it didn't change the reality of their impoverished lives.

"If it hadn't been for Momma, we would've starved," John said, recalling how his mother raised chickens to sell the eggs and churned milk for the butter. Among the possessions I have from my grandmother is an undated sheet of paper torn from a spiral notebook and labeled "Egg Money." Then it lists months and sales: Feb. $20.00, Mar. $25.16, April, $33.81, May, $41.35, June, $27.90, July $26.40, Aug. $10.00. It came to $184.62 for seven months of work.[79]

A poignant recollection of Ella Mae, Ray, and John occurred in the Busby home when the three siblings heard a terrible crash in the kitchen. The youthful trio rushed to the back of the house and found their mother sitting in a chair, her head in her palms, sobbing over the kitchen floor white with milk. Ora had placed several one-gallon buckets of milk on the end of the center-pedestal dining table to skim off the cream. The weight of the loaded pails had toppled the table, splashing milk across the wooden floor. Ora just bawled and bawled over her carelessness. Contrary to the old adage, there was indeed a time to cry over spilled milk, especially when it took food out of your family's mouths.[80]

For all his good qualities, Press was a poor financial manager. His youngest son John explained, "Dad was my role model when it came to handling money. Whatever he did, I did the opposite." It didn't help their relationship when John worked for a dollar a day chopping cotton for a Busby neighbor, and his money turned up missing. John kept his earnings in a sock in his dresser drawer and came home one day to add another dollar to his cache of thirteen when he realized his savings had disappeared. When he asked his father about it, Press told him he took it, and as long as John stayed in his house the money belonged to him. For the rest of his ninety-four years, Dad trusted only himself with money and squirreled his earnings away for whatever hard times lay ahead. Dad, too, took money from my brother's and my ten-cent-an-hour wages, but instead of using it himself, he opened a savings account in each of our names. By the time we headed to college, we both had enough money to buy a new car, me a 1968 butternut yellow Chevelle Malibu for $2,453.30. Even after buying the car, my savings exceeded a thousand dollars. Like his work ethic, Dad instilled in us the value of setting money aside for the future.[81]

By the time Press moved from Blackwell to Busby, his three oldest daughters had left home. Myrt had gotten married. Oldest child Mildred departed in 1933 to work in Snyder as a nanny. A year later, her sister Marie, who worked with the Texas Relief Commission in Sweetwater, secured Mildred a job as a case worker with the agency. "Between us we were able to get Dad out of his financial bind," Mildred recalled. They also helped their mother. At night the two sisters made and embroidered pillowcases, then bought sheets, bedspreads, towels and wash cloths for their mom. "Mother had done without for so long that she simply needed everything you could think of … We got clothes for all the family and some toys for the little brothers and sisters. In short we had a ball." In 1934 Mildred and Marie provided their siblings the only true Christmas they ever had. Marie recalled, "We have had some wonderful Christmases since, but none will ever surpass that one for Mildred and me."[82]

The final family tragedy struck in September 1942. On the first day of his senior year in high school, John with Juanita said goodbye to their mother and headed off to begin a new academic year in Sweetwater. Before lunch, they were summoned to the office and told that Ora had died. It was the second breath of death that had blown across their young lives, and it left their father rudderless. "Dad still needed Mother's counseling," Mildred said, and she was right. A year later, Press married again and his new wife made it clear she wasn't interested in having Press's kids around the house. John and Juanita were on their own then, just like their older siblings.[83]

Just as tenant farming had worn out my grandmother, it had exhausted itself between its peak in 1930 and the end of World War II. During the Depression acreage limitations implemented by the Federal government in 1934 to reduce production and boost prices, decreased the land available for tenant farmers and their families. The gathering war clouds drew farm workers to the cities in search of better paying jobs with futures. To meet wartime manpower needs, the federal government signed the Mexican Farm Labor Program Agreement with Mexico in 1942 to use migrant farmworkers in the fields along the southern border of the United States. The bracero program, as it was called, continued through 1964, reducing the need for farm families to harvest their own crops. Most importantly, mechanization of the tedious cotton-picking process loomed on the horizon. Texas farmers on the South Plains had experimented with raking over mature cotton plants with a set of prongs attached to a sled pulled by a team to clip the fiber-filled bolls from the plant. Though the primitive process reduced the labor required for harvest, the savings were offset by reduced fiber quality due to all the "trash" in the seed cotton. Although several inventors and manufacturers had toyed with mechanical pickers most lacked the capital to produce them commercially until 1942 when the International Harvester Corporation announced a barbed spindle picker was ready for production. Restrictions on the use of steel for non-war purposes prevented the commercial production of the harvester until after World War II. Gradually, the mechanical harvester took over a hand process that had changed little for centuries and, as a result, fields with tenant families pulling tow sacks down a cotton row gradually faded into history.[84]

By the end of World War II, N.P. Lewis had moved to Sweetwater, putting his farming days in the past. In 1945 when he left the country for town, 60 percent of the state's 384,977 farms still lacked electricity, 64 percent were without running water and 83 percent needed telephones. By contrast 67 percent boasted radios, powered either by wind chargers or batteries.[85] N.P. would marry three times after Ora's death and finances remained a problem. After remarrying the first time and leaving the farm, Press worked as a mechanic at Davis Farm Equipment in Sweetwater. His 1950 tax return showed he earned $2,839.24 for the year and paid $185.48 in federal taxes with charitable donations of $30 to the Baptist church, the Red Cross, and the polio fund. He drove a used 1949 Ford Tudor that cost him

$1,098, paid out in 15 monthly payments. By 1955 he was working as a custodian for the Sweetwater Independent School District at a reduced salary of $2,205.25. Shortly after that, he and his second wife divorced. He lived for a while with his various children, including our family, then moved to Weatherford to stay with Juanita before marrying again and resuming work as a school custodian. He outlived his third wife and married a final time in 1967 after he had retired.[86]

When considering his fourth marriage in 1967, he responded to Ella Mae's financial concerns, stating in a letter he and his intended bride had their Social Security, a hospital policy, her mortgage-free home and "4 or 5 thousand dollars saved up." Press noted that "Alice has quite a bit more than I do." Ultimately, health issues separated my grandfather and his last wife as both wound up in separate nursing homes attended by their children. After a series of strokes, he died in 1972. By then, his surviving offspring had grown families of their own.[87]

Mildred married Arnold McRorey of Blackwell. He worked for the county in maintenance, and she made do at home as a seamstress and quilter. "My childhood ambition was to become a great artist. I dearly loved to draw, and I wanted to paint, but as the family well knows there was no money to further our education after high school, so I guess I have satisfied myself with the creating of clothes, and there has been a lot of satisfaction in that business for me outside the money that I've earned." Though she never had children of her own, she taught children's Sunday School for seven decades at the Baptist church in Blackwell. She died in 2005.[88]

After her job with the Texas Relief Commission ended, Marie used some of her earnings to buy a third of a grocery store in Blackwell, but after Carl Preston died, she sold her interest and moved to Busby to care for her mother. She met and later married Ralph Ammons of Fisher County in May 1939. They were dining with Ora and Press on the Sunday of Pearl Harbor. "That was a solemn evening," Marie recalled. "I went to bed early, rather depressed as Ralph was a very ripe age for the draft. He came in soon after and gave me a good talking, saying he had more to fight for and defend than any of the single men." Ammons volunteered for the Army Air Corps and trained pilots in the states before being discharged as a captain in 1947. He and Marie moved to Roby and had two daughters and a son. He operated a propane/butane dealership in Roby, and she managed a flower shop for many years. Marie died in 2002.[89]

Myrt lived out her life with Bill McRorey on his family place next to the cotton fields where they first courted. They had a son and two daughters. Bill ran livestock and dryland farmed most of his life while Myrt worked as a cook many years in the cafeteria at the Blackwell school. Her scrumptious cinnamon rolls remained the favorite sweet at the Lewis family reunions for decades. Myrt died in 2008.[90]

Carl Preston lies beside his mother in Sweetwater Cemetery. Likely no one who ever knew him is alive today. Since his 1937 death, he lives only in the names of two nephews he never met.

Ella Mae never cared for the classroom, but she loved "every kind of ball," playing basketball, tennis, volleyball, and even softball on Sweetwater teams after her marriage. Born between the oldest and two youngest boys, she held her own against them. One of the great unanswered questions in my mind was how good an athlete was she? Was she a "Babe" Didrikson Zaharias-quality athlete with Olympic potential or just a solid female athlete? Even if she had been a top-tier athlete, her parents would never have known how to exploit that talent. Though she dreamed of marrying a cowboy husband, she was courted by local farm boy Joe Whitworth, who took her to a café on one date. It was the first time she had ever eaten in a restaurant. They married on Christmas Eve in 1940. He worked on the railroad early in their marriage, then went into windmill repair and water-well drilling until he retired. Joe had the roughest hands of any man I ever met, and he pestered all his nieces and nephews to the point he became their favorite uncle. He never wanted children of his own, so they had none. Ella Mae died in 2005.[91]

Ray Franklin quit high school to help on the farm after his

mother took ill. After a year of that, he sought a job where he could make more money and went to a sheet metal school in Dallas. "My greatest desire was to get a job making $200 a month, $50 a week," Ray said. "I thought if I could do that for about ten years I would just retire as rich as I could be."[92]

Before he made his "fortune," World War II intervened, and Ray enlisted in the Army in 1943. On leave he married Maxine Staton in January 1944, and five months later he landed on Omaha Beach in Normandy with the 552nd Anti-Aircraft Artillery (Automatic Weapons) Battalion. "Without a doubt that first night on the beach was the most frightening night I ever spent in my life. ... I was laying on my stomach (in a foxhole) and I was so scared it literally felt like I was shaking so bad I was bouncing on the ground."[93]

When American troops with the First U.S. Army captured the Ludendorff Bridge over the Rhine into Germany in the war's waning days, his battalion rushed to Remagen to protect the crossing from Axis aircraft trying to destroy it. The 552nd arrived at the bridge about 9 p.m. to cross over into Germany. "I'll never forget crawling on my hands and knees in front of the truck feeling—it was dark—for holes in the bridge and trying to direct the No. 1 gun crew, which was my gun crew, and the No. 2 crew across the bridge. ... With a flashlight that had just a little narrow light ... I crawled that bridge ... It was probably about 300 yards, the best I remember, but it seemed like it was two miles."[94]

He survived the war unscathed from combat and returned to Maxine, living first in Dallas then in Sweetwater where he worked at the Lone Star Cement Plant at Maryneal, then moving to Midlothian with Texas Industries. He and his wife had two sons and a daughter. When he retired as plant manager in Midlothian, he moved to De Leon and bought a place near a 552nd buddy. Ray's taped recollections totaled 33,455 words, 73 percent of them devoted to his World War II experience and aftermath. He told me once, "You got a university education, Preston. World War II was my college." He died in 1993.[95]

John left home soon after his mother died, graduating from high school and working for the U.S. Gypsum plant where his father had worked during a rough Depression year, then at a

Texaco gas station before, ironically, taking employment at the International Harvester warehouse, all in Sweetwater. Though he had been born blind in his left eye and exempted from military service, he felt he should serve his country in the war effort and joined the Merchant Marines, making thirteen trans-Atlantic trips between 1945 and 1947. Upon discharge, he returned to International Harvester in Sweetwater until taking a job as a parts man at the IH dealership in Abilene in 1949. There he met and married Jurdene Gentry that same year. In 1953 he moved to Midland as parts manager for Wes-Tex Equipment Co. When he arrived, parts sales were $10,000 a month, but by the time he left the parts business in 1974 he was selling more than $250,000 in parts a month. He provided my brother and me the college education he had always wanted. Marc and I began our professional lives debt-free with bachelor's degrees from Baylor University because of him.[96]

From Midland he returned Mom to the Abilene area in 1975, buying a quarter section of land near Hodges from Mom's aunt and building his dream home there. Despite his childhood vow not to farm cotton, he did just that for two decades before leasing the land out. He also planted sixty pecan trees and sold pecans until he left the place. He lived there forty-six years, including two years after we put Mom in a San Angelo assisted-living facility near where I lived. In 2019 Dad could no longer manage by himself, so my brother and I moved him to San Angelo to be with Mom. The hardest thing Marc and I ever had to do was sell the place that he loved dearly. He prided himself in being a landowner instead of a tenant. In one of God's great mercies, Dad died the day before we were to put him in a dementia facility in December 2020. We had cotton bolls added to the wreath on his casket the day we buried him.[97]

Juanita Myrle, the baby of the family, died the next month. She, too, left home shortly after her mother passed, getting a job with the state hospital in Big Spring and working in the kitchen as a supervisor. The hospital hosted a monthly dance where she met Hoyle Nix, the leader of his West Texas Cowboys band. Nix in 1949 composed the country song *Big Balls in Cowtown*, later made popular by Bob Wills. Juanita impressed Nix with her piano playing and took a side job playing music on weekends in his band, one night at a VFW hall raking in $13 in tips "which was the most I ever got and to me was quite a bit" of money. Juanita said, "I must admit that would have been my life had it not been for the places we went to play music. But I love good music and enjoyed it for about six or eight months." Ultimately, she met Walter Roberts, an Army veteran from the Pacific theater, and they married, living in Weatherford and the Fort Worth area most of their lives. They had three sons. Like Dad, she too suffered from dementia before her 2021 death.[98]

As I write this some six months after her passing, I find it hard to believe those who had played such an integral part in establishing my view of life, family, and work are all gone. As brothers, Marc and I used to joke that we didn't have friends growing up, just family that we visited every chance we got. At our mother's suggestion the clan in 1951 initiated an annual Lewis Family Reunion that continued each summer through 2007, when only Myrt, Dad and Juanita survived. My generation found it impossible to continue the gatherings due to distance and conflicting schedules of our own grown children and grandchildren. The reunion died away like our parents and the farm tenancy/crop lien system.

Even so, cotton made my family, just like it shaped Texas in the first century of its existence, even if the ranching industry surpassed it in legend and the petroleum industry overtook it in wealth. As a result, the tenant farmers and sharecroppers, whether white, black or brown, walk anonymously through the pages of Texas history, their contributions overlooked at best or demeaned at worst.

Dad and his siblings were salt-of-the-earth people, remnants of a generation of Texans that has almost faded away. While they may have lacked urban sophistication and extensive education, they were not morons, the learned Edward Everett Davis notwithstanding. They shared a wisdom that comes from living close to the earth and a work ethic that comes from tilling the soil. They suffered through the hardships of the Great Depression, ached through the tragedies of family and World War II, and overcame their disadvantaged upbringing. They may have been casualties of economic forces beyond their control, but they never saw themselves as victims. They seldom complained about the lives they were born into, but were determined to make a better life for themselves and their children. Hard work and common sense—spawned by their years of toil in the hot, dusty cotton fields of West Texas—went a long way to accomplishing their goals, even with their limited educations. Perhaps they didn't aim high enough, but their opportunities were constrained by the narrowness of their vision beyond a cotton field. Even so, they never let their educational deficiencies prevent them from remaining devoted to their spouses, respecting their country and its flag, or raising decent law-abiding, God-fearing children. Despite the challenges of hard times and losses, the family endured and left a quiet legacy of decency.

"My memories of childhood, I know, seem to always be happy ones," Ray said. "We certainly didn't have a lot, but there was a lot of love, and the boys and the girls seemed to get along good."[99]

"As a family," Mildred said, "we were very poor in material wealth but very wealthy in the things that really count, for we never lacked for love, understanding, and family fun. Dad was no manager as I've already said, but he would have given any of us the very shirt off his back or the last dollar he had if he thought we needed it."[100]

The problem was Press seldom had a dollar to give. When he died in 1972, each of his children contributed $60 apiece to pay for his burial. At the time of his death, his belongings—other than his clothes—fit into a shoe box. My dad could not believe that a man could spend seventy-nine years on this earth and not accumulate more than that, but the inverse lessons Press taught his son, meant that Dad saved, scrimped and invested cautiously. He died with more assets than he could ever have imagined when he was chopping and picking cotton in West Texas.

In his remarks at Dad's graveside service, Marc listed two dozen adjectives to describe our father. Among those descriptive words, he used "frugal" three times. As Marc said, when the Sears Catalog offered good, better or best, Dad always bought good. Even so, the cheapest Sears had to offer was better than

what he had grown up with.

When concluding Dad's eulogy on December 14, 2020, I picked up a dustpan I had taken from his hearth when we sold his and Mom's house. The dustpan was the last item I removed before turning the keys over to the new owner. Dad had crafted the implement from an old broom handle, a block of wood, a few wood screws, a couple pieces of duct tape and an expired New Mexico license plate he had kept from a vehicle when he built a cabin in Ruidoso.

Holding up the dustpan in that country cemetery for his family and friends to see, I said it perfectly illustrated Dad's life because "he always made the best out of whatever God gave him."

The same can be said for the members of his family and his generation: They were resilient, and they made the best out of what Texas provided them. And, Texas is a better place because of them.

N.P. Lewis Family Reunion, Blackwell, Texas, 1951

Endnotes:

1 Ella Mae Whitworth Memoirs, 1978, (Author's collection).

2 John Bracken Lewis Memoirs, 1974, (Author's collection).

3 *The Texas Almanac and State Industrial Guide, 1926*, p. 135.

4 Eugene C. Barker, *The Life of Stephen F. Austin: Founder of Texas, 1793-1836*, (Austin, University of Texas Press, 1926, Fourth Paperback Edition, 1990), pp. 124, 371; and *The Texas Almanac and State Industrial Guide, 1925*, p. 109-10; Karen Gerhardt Britton, "Cotton Ginning," *Handbook of Texas Online*, accessed May 19, 2021, https://www.tshaonline.org/handbook/entries/cotton-ginning; *The Texas Almanac and State Industrial Guide, 1927*, p. 136; *The Texas Almanac and State Industrial Guide, 1933*, p. 149; *The Texas Almanac and State Industrial Guide, 1929*, p. 97; *The Texas Almanac and State Industrial Guide, 1931*, p. 136; Tony D. Williams, Texas Cotton Ginners' Association, "Number of Cotton Gins and Number of Bales of Cotton Ginned for Texas: 1900-1984" p.1; Sven Beckert, *Empire of Cotton: A Global History* (New York, Vintage Books, 2014), p. 353; U.S. Department of Agriculture National Agricultural Statistics Service, accessed May 11, 2021, https://www.nass.usda.gov/Quick_Stats/Ag_Overview/stateOverview.php?state=TEXAS; and Tony D. Williams, Texas Cotton Ginners' Association, e-mail, May 18, 2021

5 Neil Foley, *The White Scourge: Mexicans, Blacks, and Poor Whites in Texas Cotton Culture*, (Berkeley/Los Angeles, University of California Press, 1997), p. 6.

6 Edward Everett Davis, *The White Scourge*, (San Antonio, The Naylor Company, 1940, Kessinger Legacy Reprints), pp. ix-x; *The Texas Almanac and State Industrial Guide, 1937*, p. 24; and *The Texas Almanac and State Industrial Guide,1941-42*, p. 201.

7 George Sessions Perry, *Hold Autumn in Your Hand*, (New York, Curtis Brown, Ltd., 1941; Albuquerque, University of New Mexico Press, 1969, fifth paperbound printing,1994), pp. 251-60; Maxine Hairston, "Perry, George Sessions," *Handbook of Texas Online,* accessed May 01, 2021, https://www.tshaonline.org/handbook/entries/perry-george-sessions, published by the Texas State Historical Association; and Don Graham, "Literature," *Handbook of Texas Online*, accessed May 05, 2021, https://www.tshaonline.org/handbook/entries/literature, published by the Texas State Historical Association.

8 Stephen Yafa, *Big Cotton: How a Humble Fiber Created Fortunes, Wrecked Civilizations and Put America on the Map*, (New York, Viking, 2004; New York, Penguin Books, 2006, published as *Cotton: The Biography of a Revolutionary Fiber*), pp. 1-4.

9 *The Texas Almanac and State Industrial Guide, 1927*, p. 136.

10 Letter, Ora Lewis to Myrt, et al, June 3, 1941

11 Rebecca Sharpless, *Fertile Ground, Narrow Choices: Women on Texas Cotton Farms, 1900-1940*, (Chapel Hill, University of North Carolina Press, 1999), pp. 8, 12.

12 High School Pass Book and Promotion/Graduation Certificate, The Plano Public School, June 17, 1904 (Author's Collection), p. 5.

13 Marriage License, Mr. Press Lewis and Miss Ora Garrett, Clerk, County Court, Collin County, issued Sept. 27, 1911, G.E. Strother.

14 Mildred Ruth Lewis McRorey Memoirs, 1974 (Author's Collection); and *Texas Almanac, 1943-1944*, p. 138.

15 Mildred McRorey Memoirs.

16 Mildred McRorey Memoirs.

17 Sharpless, p. 39.

18 Marie Lewis Ammons Memoirs, 1979, (Author's Collection); and Mildred McRorey Memoirs.

19 *Texas Almanac, 2016-2017*, p. 363; and Gerald McDaniel, "Nolan County," Handbook of Texas Online, accessed May 14, 2021, https://www.tshaonline.org/handbook/entries/nolan-county

20 Mildred McRorey Memoirs.

21 Thad Sitton and Dan K. Utley, *From Can See to Can't: Texas Cotton Farmers on the Southern Prairies* (Austin, 1997), p. 10; Tony D. Williams, Texas Cotton Ginners' Association, "Number of Cotton Gins and Number of Bales of Cotton Ginned for Texas: 1900-1984" p.1; and *The Texas Almanac and State Industrial Guide, 1928,* p. 205.

22 *The Texas Almanac and State Industrial Guide, 1941-1942,* p. 207; and National Agriculture Statistical Service, United States Department of Agriculture website, https://www.nass.usda.gov/Quick_Stats/Ag_Overview/stateOverview .php?state=TEXAS, accessed May 14, 2021.

23 John Bracken Lewis Memoirs; and Mildred McRorey Memoirs.

24 Sharpless, p. 9.

25 John Lewis Memoirs; *Texas Almanac, 2016-2017*, p. 292; and Hooper Shelton, "Fisher County," Handbook of Texas Online, accessed May 14, 2021, https://www.tshaonline.org/handbook/entries/fisher-county.

26 Sitton and Utley, p. 46; Sharpless, p. 7; and John Lewis Memoirs.

27 Cecil Harper, Jr. and E. Dale Odom, "Farm Tenancy," *Handbook of Texas Online,* accessed May 05, 2021, https://www.tshaonline.org/handbook/entries/farm-tenancy, published by the Texas State Historical Association; Gilbert C. Fite: Southern Agriculture, 1865-1980 (Lexington, University of Kentucky Press, 1984), pp. 234-35; and *Texas Almanac, 1943-44*, p. 141.

28 Mildred McRorey Memoirs; and Edna Myrtle Lewis McRorey Memoirs, 1979, (Author's Collection).

29 Mildred McRorey Memoirs.

30 Agricultural Statistics, 1936, U.S. Department of Agriculture, U.S. Government Printing Office, 1936, pp. 75-76; and Agricultural

Statistics, 1950, U.S. Department of Agriculture, U.S. Government Printing Office, 1950, p. 68.

31 Mildred McRorey Memoirs; and Myrtle McRorey Memoirs.

32 Marie Ammons Memoirs; and Myrtle McRorey Memoirs.

33 John Lewis Memoirs; and Myrtle McRorey Memoirs.

34 John Lewis Memoirs.

35 Sitton and Utley, 55.

36 John Lewis Memoirs; and Mildred McRorey Memoirs.

37 Mildred McRorey Memoirs; and Sharpless, p. 120.

38 Mildred McRorey Memoirs.

39 John Lewis Memoirs.

40 Mildred McRorey Memoirs; and Juanita Myrle Lewis Roberts Memoirs, 1980, (Author's Collection).

41 Ray Franklin Lewis Memoirs, 1984 (Author's Collection); John Lewis Memoirs; and Mildred McRorey Memoirs.

42 Ella Mae Lewis Whitworth Memoirs (Author's Collection); Ray Lewis Memoirs; and John Lewis Memoirs.

43 *Texas Almanac and Industrial Guide 1929*, p. 99; *Texas Almanac and Industrial Guide 1936*, p. 238; Ella Mae Whitworth Memoirs; and John Lewis Memoirs.

44 Mildred McRorey Memoirs; https://www.usinflationcalculator.com/; and 2021 Federal Poverty Guidelines Chart (Effective Jan. 13, 2021), https://www.medicaidplanningassistance.org/federal-poverty-guidelines/, accessed May 20, 2021.

45 Texas Almanac and State Industrial Guide, 1933, p. 148; and *Texas Almanac, 1945-1946*, p. 189-90.

46 John Lewis Memoirs.

47 John Lewis Memoirs; Myrtle McRorey Memoirs; and *The Texas Almanac and State Industrial Guide,1936*, p. 237.

48 John Lewis Memoirs; and *The Texas Almanac and State Industrial Guide,1928*, p. 198-99.

49 John Lewis Memoirs; and Sitton and Utley, p. 158.

50 Marie Ammons Memoirs.

51 Sharpless, p. 175-79.

52 John Lewis Memoirs.

53 John Lewis Memoirs; Sharpless, p. 181; Ella Mae Whitworth Memoirs; and *The Texas Almanac and State Industrial Guide,1945-46*, p. 190.

54 Sitton and Utley, p. 209; and John Lewis Memoirs.

55 John Lewis Memoirs; and Mildred McRorey Memoirs.

56 Ella Mae Whitworth Memoirs.

57 N.P. Lewis Family oral tradition.

58 Ella Mae Whitworth Memoirs.

59 Ella Mae Lewis to Mildred McRorey, Nov. 1, 1935; John Lewis to Mildred McRorey, Nov. 1, 1935; and Ora Lewis to Mildred McRorey, Oct. 31, 1935 (Author's Collection).

60 Myrtle McRorey Memoirs.

61 Mildred McRorey Memoirs.
62 John Lewis Memoirs; "Roby Springs 13-7 Upset on Colorado," *Abilene Reporter-News*, p. 10, Nov. 20, 1937; and "Roby Football Player Is Dead," *Abilene Reporter-News*, p. 1, Nov. 26, 1937.
63 John Lewis Memoirs.
64 Mildred McRorey Memoirs.
65 Carl Preston Lewis Collection (Author's Collection).
66 Mildred McRorey Memoirs.
67 Myrtle McRorey Memoirs.
68 Myrtle McRorey Memoirs.
69 Mildred McRorey Memoirs; and John Lewis Memoirs.
70 Mildred McRorey Memoirs.
71 Mildred McRorey Memoirs; Myrtle McRorey Memoirs; Ella Mae Whitworth Memoirs; and Juanita Roberts Memoirs.
72 Mildred McRorey Memoirs.
73 Ella Mae Whitworth Memoirs.
74 Ella Mae Whitworth Memoirs; and Ray Lewis Memoirs.
75 John Lewis Memoirs.
76 Ray Lewis Memoirs; Mildred McRorey Memoirs;
77 Ella Mae Whitworth Memoirs.
78 Ray Lewis Memoirs.
79 John Lewis Memoirs; and undated list of egg revenue (Author's Collection).
80 John Lewis Memoirs; and Ella Mae Whitworth Memoirs.
81 John Lewis Memoirs.
82 Mildred McRorey Memoirs; and Marie Ammons Memoirs.
83 John Lewis Memoirs; and Mildred McRorey Memoirs.
84 Fred L. Koestler, "Bracero Program," *Handbook of Texas Online*, accessed September 06, 2021, https://www.tshaonline.org/handbook/entries/bracero-program, Published by the Texas State Historical Association; and *Texas Almanac and State Industrial Guide, 1929*, p. 98; Donald Holley, "John Daniel Rust (1892–1954)", Encyclopedia of Arkansas online, https://encyclopediaofarkansas.net/entries/john-daniel-rust-2272/ accessed May 22, 2021, University of Arkansas at Monticello
85 *Texas Almanac,1947-48,* p. 195.
86 John Lewis Memoirs; Juanita Roberts Memoirs; 1950 U.S. Individual Income Tax Return, Feb. 6, 1951 (Author's Collection); and 1955 U.S. Individual Income Tax Return, Feb. 11, 1956 (Author's Collection).
87 Letter, N.P. Lewis to Ella Mae Whitworth, Sept. 27, 1967.
88 Mildred McRorey Memoirs.
89 Marie Ammons Memoirs.
90 Myrtle McRorey Memoirs.
91 Ella Mae Whitworth Memoirs.
92 Ray Lewis Memoirs.

93 Ray Lewis Memoirs.
94 Ray Lewis Memoirs.
95 Ray Lewis Memoirs.
96 John Lewis Memoirs.
97 John Lewis Memoirs.
98 Juanita Roberts Memoirs.
99 Ray Lewis Memoirs.
100 Mildred McRorey Memoirs.

CHAPTER TWO

Cotton-Picking Folks

What follows are the recollections of seven children of a Texas tenant farmer, first in North Texas and later in West Texas during a span that started with World War I, continued during the Roaring Twenties, evolved into the Great Depression and ended with World War II. My father, uncle and five aunts were not highly educated, so their grammar and syntax were not sophisticated. I have corrected obvious spelling errors, grammar mistakes that I thought were distracting to a reader and syntax issues when rearranging words or a few sentences added to the clarity of their recollections. Occasionally, I added a word or phrase for clarification in brackets. Even so, I've tried to keep the substance of their memoirs true to their handwritten or tape-recorded memories because I felt they talked more eloquently about their lives in their own way than a strictly edited version would convey.

To maintain the integrity of their recollections, I have kept them in their entirety, even when I quoted individual sections in my preceding eulogy. The only exception is with Ray Franklin's recollections related to World War II. Since those sections, while fascinating, were not germane to Depression life on a Texas tenant farm, I have excised them for publication in a later book on Ray's and my father's experiences in World War II. Over the years, Dad would periodically have a thought about the old days and jot it down for me. I have incorporated those additions in his section where appropriate and on occasion moved paragraphs around for topical coherence.

Their stories were told when they approached their fifties and sixties, so the vagaries of time and age may have colored their recollections and clouded their memories, especially when it came to dates and years. Where they have mentioned a date that I could prove erroneous, I corrected it, but otherwise left it alone. It has been forty or more years since I collected these accounts. Some anecdotes may seem insensitive by today's standards, but I have left them in to give the true tenor of the times.

The N.P. Lewises remained a close-knit family, holding annual reunions for more than a half century beginning in 1951. With parents and eight children, they were a large family, but actually smaller than the family N.P. Lewis, my grandfather, was born into. His family eventually included a dozen siblings, as best I can determine. My grandmother had two brothers and two sisters. My grandparents' brothers and sisters and some of their children meander through these accounts. I had trouble enough keeping up with who was who as a kid, so it remains confusing to this day with no surviving aunts or uncles to clarify the relationships for me. Rather than try to provide long explanations of those kinships, I have left the names with the expectation that the reader would accept that they are kinfolks, usually aunts and uncles or cousins.

I have, however, provided below a list of my grandparents and their children's names along with the names of their eventual spouses to acquaint the reader with the family. Additionally, I have included a listing of the nicknames that the children assumed during their youth, as they sometimes show up in the accounts. Even at family reunions decades later, the siblings would often refer to each other by their nicknames, some of known origins and others of murkier pasts.

Because of the itinerant nature of tenant farming during the Great Depression, I have produced a list of the years and the places the family lived between 1912 and 1944 to help the reader with the chronology as the family grew and moved from farm to farm.

As the siblings provided me their "memoirs" over the course of a decade, they came in no certain order. Rather than publish them in the order I received them, I decided to list them in the birth order as much as anything to establish the family hierarchy.

Consequently, readers will see references to some "memoirs" that they have yet to read.

This project has been a labor of love because these are the stories that made up the folklore of my family as told by my father and his siblings. As they are all gone now, I did not want those stories to be lost to future generations. I remember as a child often opting to sit with my dad and his siblings to listen to their stories rather than go outside and play with my cousins. My hope is the reader will enjoy these tales today as much as I did as a kid.

N.P. Lewis Family
1912-1944

Parents
Noah Preston Lewis, 1893-1972
Ora Bell Garrett, 1886-1942

Children
Mildred Ruth Lewis, 1912-2005
    (Spouse: Arnold McRorey)
Grace Marie Lewis, 1913-2002
    (Spouse: Ralph Ammons)
Edna Myrtle Lewis, 1915-2008
    (Spouse: Bill McRorey)
Carl Preston Lewis, 1921-1937
Ella Mae Lewis, 1922-2005
    (Spouse: Joe Whitworth)
Ray Franklin Lewis, 1923-1993
    (Spouse: Maxine Staton)
John Bracken Lewis, 1926-2020
    (Spouse: Jurdene Gentry)
Juanita Myrle Lewis, 1928-2021
    (Spouse: Walter Roberts)

Family Nicknames
Mildred Ruth: Deduse
Grace Marie: Ree or Santa
Edna Myrtle: Myrt
Carl: Bucky or Buck
Ella Mae: Eller, Tis or Titter
Ray: Pete
John: J.B., Jabe or Jaber
Juanita: Puss or Honey

Ella Mae, John, Mildred, N.P., Juanita, Ray, Myrt and Marie, circa 1943

Family Residences
1912: Allen, Collin County, Texas
1913-14: Plano, Collin County, Texas
1915-24: Seagoville, Dallas County, Texas—Lived on three
      different farms.

1924: Nolan County, Texas—Resided last three months of the year with N.P. Lewis's brother and family.

1925: Wastella, Nolan County, Texas—Moved 1.5 miles east of Wastella, some 7 miles north of Roscoe for the year.

1926-29: Nolan County, Texas—Relocated 3 miles south of Roscoe on the Forrester place.

1930-31: Nolan County, Texas—Moved 4 miles north of Roscoe to the Younger place.

1932: Nolan County, Texas—Relocated 3 miles northwest of Roscoe to Woodard place.

1933-34: Blackwell, Nolan County, Texas—Moved to Copeland place west of town.

1935-43: Busby, Fisher County, Texas—Relocated to C.H. Bolin place.

1944: Nolan County, Texas—Moved north of Sweetwater to Scott place; rented home, but did not farm.

1945: Sweetwater, Nolan County, Texas—Resided at 611 N. Ninth St.

CHAPTER THREE

Mildred Ruth Lewis McRorey

When I look back over my sixty-two years, it is indeed with a lot of fond memories, memories which revolve around a large family that had to work very hard for a living, but with so much love for each other that it helped soft-pedal the hard work for an existence. Each one in the family had to do their share, and I think it caused our respect to grow for each other, and we always knew we had the love and respect of our dad and mother. Dad never sent us to work alone unless he had another job to do somewhere else. Dad was a big fellow, six-foot-two inches, and a hard worker. I thought there was nothing he could not do.

Growing up on a farm in the late teens, twenties and thirties certainly was not an easy time in history. The Great Depression really taught all of us growing up during that period of time how to exist with such a little portion of this world's goods and how to stretch and stretch everything.

I remember so well how Mother would take such pleasure out of preparing a simple dish into something rather exotic while we were in the field at work, and how her eyes would light when we ate with such gusto and asked how she did it. It was truly amazing the delicious meals she could prepare out of almost nothing. To this day, I can just taste the delicious home-grown fried potatoes, milk gravy, some bacon if we had it, hot biscuits, homemade cow butter and syrup for supper. Also, Dad always had some meat hogs to butcher in the fall of each year and, oh my, what a delight when it came time to do that.

Our first meal from the hogs was fried liver, milk gravy with hot biscuits and the traditional sorghum syrup. As soon as Dad gutted the hogs, he would cut out the melts (spleen) and give them to us kids to roast on the fire around the old wash pots where they heated the water to scald the hogs in order to remove the hair. I never did care much for that roasted melt, but we always roasted it anyway. Oh, yes, and another thing, he always cut out the bladders, and we would get a hollow straw and blow those stinking things up for balloons and balls. They really made good volleyballs and would last a long time and get blacker and blacker as they collected more and more dirt, but we had fun playing with them.

Dad was a real artist at trimming and preparing the meat to cure out. Then, of course, there was the sausage to grind and sack in homemade sacks made from the flour sacks. It was not an easy job to put all that meat through the old sausage mill either, but a cake of sausage in a biscuit made the best sandwich ever in our school lunches. (However, the real icing on the cake for our lunches—or anytime for that matter—was biscuit dough rolled out neatly then spread with plenty of butter, sugar, and cinnamon, rolled over and baked into the most delicious butter roll you ever ate.) Then the fat from the hogs had to be rendered into lard out in the old wash pots and stored away in five- and ten-gallon lard stands. The cracklings were then used to make lye soap to do the family laundry; we also used it to shampoo our hair for we simply did not have anything else. When the hams, shoulders, and sides of bacon were all cured out, they were sacked and hung from the rafters of the smokehouse. This meat would last for quite awhile, but not quite all year.

Dad was the oldest son of a large farm family. Mother grew up in the small town of Plano, Texas, and her father was a carpenter. Dad's family did not practice economy like mother was taught to do, so she was the one in our family who had to keep her foot on the brake, economy wise, for a dollar to Dad was to spend and not to worry about whether he would need it worse for something more important the next day or month, but Mother looked ahead.

Dad and Mother married September 28, 1911, in McKinney, Texas, and lived with Grandpa and Grandma Lewis the first year of their married life. That was quite a change for Mother, as she had two sisters and two brothers (She lost a little sister "Ruth" when quite young that I was named for), and she had been teaching school eight years before she and Dad married. In those years, when you finished high school you could go to Summer Normal and get a teacher's certificate and teach school the next fall and that is what Mother did. I think Mother really loved teaching.

Grandpa Lewis (Jacob Mills Lewis) and all his family were Baptist and very strict in most ways. Mother and Dad told about going to a party in the community shortly after they were married where they played some ring plays *[Games played in a circle with dance movements and singing]*, and they had such a good time. When they got home and went upstairs to their room, Aunt Vevy (Dad's sister, just older than him) came up to their room and really ate them out for going to a dance. Mother was a member of the First Christian Church, and to me she was the most understanding Christian and so broad-minded about everything. Grandpa Lewis hurt her feelings many times by making slight remarks about her church (or that is as if she were a Church of Christ Campbellite as he called it). The First Christian had music and Sunday School just like the Baptists with very little difference in their beliefs. Mother managed to keep her feelings to herself and say nothing.

I was born while they lived with Grandpa and Grandma Lewis, August 13, 1912, at Allen, Texas. The next year Dad and Mother moved to Plano, Texas, and Dad worked in a harness shop (that was long before tractor days) for a Mr. J.T. Horn. In those days horse power was truly horse power, for they did the farm work with horses and mules so there was a great demand for leather harnesses for the animals. In fact all the time I was home, Dad farmed with teams and did not get a tractor until after I left home.

Mother had a house and lot here at Plano that she bought and paid for with her school teaching money, and when they moved to Plano, Dad persuaded Mother to put her place in on a larger one that they shared with Grandpa and Grandma Robbins (Dad's mother's parents), and in no time at all the grandparents wound up with the whole thing, and Mother was always so bitter about that deal, more so perhaps because she overheard the grandparents planning just how they would beat Dad and Mother out of their part. I think this experience caused Mother to be more forceful in teaching us children to not only deal fairly with each other but also with our fellow man. Another thing I remember hearing Dad and Mother talk about happened while we lived in Plano. Marie was born November 2, 1913, and Dad hired a Negro lady to help Mother with the work for several weeks, and how they learned to love and appreciate her and her ability to manage as she was such a wise shopper and how nice it would have been had they been able to have kept her on to help Mother with her work and manage the grocery bill, as they thought she could make a dollar go farther than anyone they ever knew.

I'm not sure how long we lived in Plano, but we moved to Seagoville, Texas, sometime before Myrt was born on December 20, 1915, and Dad began to farm for a living. From here on I believe I remember all I shall write about for I was going on four years of age. What I remember about Myrt's entering the family is that Marie and I were taken to a close neighbor (Mr. and Mrs. Bert Moore) to spend the night, and I remember the brown oilcloth tablecloth with fish printed on it at Mrs. Moore's; then Dad coming for us the next morning and carrying us home in his arms telling us we had a new baby sister. Before I forget I must say Myrt should have had a chance to be a pianist, but we did not have a piano at that time so the old family sewing machine had to do double duty as a sewing machine, and Myrt's piano or organ because she pedaled it like an organ. It was an old treadle machine from Sears Roebuck, a "Minnesota A." She simply beat all the finish off the front cabinet with her tunes, but it did not damage the machine's ability to do the family sewing. Myrt did in later years learn to pick the guitar. J.B. tells me that Ella Mae used the window sills for her piano, and that they took the same beatings that Myrt gave the sewing machine.

Our family sang a lot together. Dad played the French-harp *[harmonica]* and picked the guitar. He fixed some kind of wire rack that fit around his neck to hold the harp so he could play it and pick the guitar at the same time. Mother had a beautiful voice; also, Marie had such a nice soprano voice. I tried my luck with alto, as that seemed to fit my range best. Myrt had the widest range of all as she could manage tenor, alto, or soprano. We all loved those family singing sessions, and as the family grew all the other brothers and sisters were good singers, and both Ella Mae and Juanita could play the piano, even Ray and J.B. managed "Chopsticks" and a few other tunes, and by this time there was a piano in the home; and Ella Mae was able to take about five months of piano lessons by Mother sending butter and eggs to the teacher, a Mrs. George. After we older girls married and would gather at home for visits, sometime during the visits we would all gather around the piano for a sing-song, religious, popular and some ballads, with Juanita and Ella Mae at the piano. Ralph (Marie's future husband), was a good singer and leader; Arnold (my future husband) could sing well, but hardly ever would; Bill (Myrt's future husband) loved it, but he could not manage a very good tune. Anyway, we had fun.

One thing that really stands out so vividly in my memory is the cyclone that blew our house away with Mother, Marie, Myrt, and me in it in 1918 at Seagoville. I do not know when Grandpa Lewis moved to Seagoville, but at the time in 1918 they lived just across a field from us, and Grandpa and Dad's brothers all traded work and helped each other with whatever needed to be done. At this time they had harvested the potato crop and were sacking the potatoes at Grandpa's barn getting ready to take them to Dallas (20 miles north) to market when the storm came. This, of course, was during World War I; and groceries were rationed; and Dad had just brought home our month's supply. When the kitchen window blew out, Mother ran to move the box of groceries and the storm separated the kitchen, which was a shed room on the main part of the house, from the part where Marie, Myrt, and I were playing jacks. Mother was blown about one hundred yards down in the field with the kitchen, and the rest of the house was blown over or wrecked on the spot where it sat. Mother made her way back to us and began to gather us up. I remember so well that something heavy was on my right hand, and it took me some

time to wiggle it out from under whatever it was. When I did, I crawled up under a wall, which was held up by an old iron bed, to get out of the rain and wind. Mother located Marie and then Myrt, and all she could see was her feet sticking up out of the wreckage. She had to move the quilt box or the sewing machine—I don't remember which—to get her loose. Myrt was lifeless, but when Mother got her out in the wind and rain, she caught her breath, just had the wind knocked out of her.

Mother said, "Let's go to Grandpa's," so we started, she carrying Myrt and leading Marie. I had to manage on my own. Never will I forget how the wind pressure was so great that I could not keep my mouth shut, and I got it full of dirt and chips, and the wind would blow me down, but I kept getting up for I knew how important it was to get to where Dad was. He came running to meet us in a few minutes for he was afraid the storm had blown us away. The Lord truly blessed us, for no one was hurt outside of scratches and bruises. They built us a new house; and I know we kids were always frightened whenever it rained for a long time after the storm; and Mother used to tell us a story about how the raindrops splattering were little people on their way to church. She had a very special way of making us feel safe.

This also was my first year in school. At that time Dad's youngest sister Opal and three younger brothers George, Roy, and Cliff were also in school, and I guess they helped look after me. I went to a three-room school (Rains Hall). My first teacher was a Miss Harvey and, of course, I thought she was the greatest. Those were happy years there in school at Rains Hall. This is the only place where I ever remember my Dad spanking me, two different times. We had to furnish our own drinking cups, and mine was a folding tin cup that Dad scratched my initials on the bottom. It came up missing one day, and I thought I knew who got it. So sure enough, in a few days I found it in the girl's coat pocket and just took it back. When I got home, Dad asked me where I found it, and I told him in the wood box. I guess he knew I wasn't telling the truth so he kept on until I told him. He said, "Okay, Mildred, I'm going to spank you for not telling me the truth where you found it; I know it is your drinking cup, but you should have told me the truth." This made quite an impression on me. The second time he spanked me I was trying to show Marie how to play hopscotch, and she was tearing up my hopscotch markings on the ground as fast as I made them. Finally, I lost my temper with her and shoved her down, and Dad, of course, saw that part of it, and he spanked me for that. I always did think Marie should have had one, too.

Marie started to school the next year. She was always smart as a tack and quick to learn. The school was built in an L shape with porches in the L, and that was our stage when we had programs. I remember Marie bringing the roof down one night with a reading she did, also another time with a skit she did with another girl (Ruth Houston). She was really good, and Dad and Mother were so proud of her. Along about this time, World War I ended; and so many of those old airplanes (the two-wing type) were brought back to Dallas Love Field; and there were days and days when the sky was so full of them. We kids were so fascinated with them that we would sit out and watch for hours.

Grandpa then moved to what they called "down in the Point," but I don't know why they called it the Point. Anyway, we then moved on to the place where Grandpa moved from. There was a big orchard and a big blackberry patch. I remember people would come on specified days to pick berries, and Dad sold them for so much a gallon. There was also a huge garden, and that is really when I learned what God meant when He put Adam and Eve out of the Garden of Eden and told Adam he would have to eat off the ground all the days of his life and cursed it with thorns and thistles (Genesis 3:17-19). We really had to put out the sweat, cutting the weeds and thistles from the orchard and garden, bugging the potato vines and working in the field. One time when we were hoeing in the orchard, we got Mother so tickled she let us quit, for we began to tell what all we had to do before night, and what really got the job done was when we told her we had to feed the asses. It really was not all that bad, for there were lots of luscious dewberries on the field fence rows which got ripe before the blackberries; big pecan trees in the fields and on what we called the slough, a branch of the Trinity River; also big persimmons which really did pucker your mouth if you tried to eat them too green. Dad also raised a lot of peanuts and bailed them into hay for stock feed; and it was just great in the winter to go out and pick off a big pan of peanuts to parch when Dad would break open a bale of hay for the horses and cows; also to pop a big pan of popcorn, which we grew, was another winter night's treat.

Dad also saved a lot of cottonseed to feed the milk cows (Mother thought that the cottonseed made the cows give much better milk and made such a good yellow butter) and also to plant his next year's cotton crop. The seed house was our favorite place to play. We built all kinds of castles and cities in the cottonseed. I cannot remember learning to milk a cow. Marie and I must have been born knowing how to milk for we had to do a lot of it, and so did the rest of the family as they came along. My, but how cold your fingers would get on a cold winter morn, but the milking had to be done before we went to school.

Carl was born August 4, 1921. We were all so proud of our little brother, and naturally Dad was elated over his first son. I was nine years old and this is when I learned to make biscuits and had to help with the family meals from there on. Ella Mae was born August 30, 1922, and she has been the belle of the family for she has kept us all in stitches with her funny expressions and stunts. To this very day, she keeps our nieces and nephews spellbound with her stories about growing up during the Depression and what all we had to do. They think she is a great story builder, but it is not as far-fetched as they think because she really is telling it about as it really was.

Ray was born November 13, 1923, and everything went nicely until he was ten months old. He got real sick, and we came so near to losing him. Aunt Stella, Dad's sister who was a registered nurse, came to nurse him through this spell of sickness. I shall never forget the day he passed the crisis. Aunt Stella gave up and fell across the bed and began to cry. Mother fell on her knees beside the bed and began to pray; big ol' Dad standing there so helpless. I thought I would choke to death. I just knew Mother's prayers were answered, for in a few minutes Ray began to rally, and we could see him getting better from then on. That was our first near tragedy in the family, but he grew up to be such a fine specimen of a man with so much wit and fun to be with. On one occasion some of the kids had been pestering him, and he hollered out, "I'm going to turn around three times, and there won't be anyone left in this room but me." He looked up and saw Dad, then added, "...and Papa."

One time there was so much rain that the Trinity River got on a big rise, and when it did the slough at the back of our place overflowed and surrounded our house and three others there on the ridge; so we all had to move out on account of the high water. I think we stayed out two weeks at Grandpa's. When we came home we had to cross what they called "the slash" in boats. Uncle George brought Marie and me across, and for the fun of it he took us around through some brush, and I never have cared for a boat ride since. They also swam the stock (cows and horses) out to protect them from the flood. However, the water never did quite get up to the houses.

While we lived here Marie, Myrt, and I really had some fancy playhouses. We would take the old black mud from the slash and mold play dishes and set them out in the sun to dry, and they were just like bricks and would last a long time. We did not know what it was like to have many store-bought toys, so we provided our own. On one occasion we dashed out to play in the playhouse right after lunch, and Mother called us to come do the dishes. We sure did hate to have to go in and do the dishes, so we decided to go to sleep and after awhile Mother's patience wore out and out she came with Dad's razor strap. Needless to say she did not have any trouble waking us up. We would try Mother until her patience wore out, then all Dad had to say was, "You heard what your mother said." That would put us moving. Another thing we did was go crawfishing off the side of the bridge across a draw in the slash. Our bait was a hunk of fat meat on a string and a gallon bucket to put our catch in. Then we would take the crawfish back to the house, pour them out on the ground and watch them crawl back toward the draw.

There were a good many neighbor kids who lived in our community, and they would come to our house lots on Sunday afternoons, and we played baseball in our big backyard. Dad always played with us.

Dad rented some land across the slough to work that he called the new ground. I think it had just been cleared of all the timber and brush and was the first time ever to have been cultivated. As I remember there were still a good many stumps to be hoed around. But the thing that would be hard for the younger members of our family to believe were the chiggers we had to contend with. They were so bad that Dad would soak rags with kerosene oil and tie around the tops of our shoes trying to keep them from getting on us so bad, and those rags would be red with those little boogers when we would get home from the field every day, and still it did not keep them from getting all over us. Marie, Myrt, and I would have a chigger-picking session; we simply laid down on the floor and picked those things off each other.

Another playhouse we had here was upstairs on the rafters. It was not sealed, so we put some planks across the rafters and got up there and made a playhouse. I remember I just loved to crawl up there and make clothes for my doll; Marie and Myrt did too. I don't think we hardly had room to turn around, but I guess that is what made it so interesting to us. The kitchen part of the house was not two-story and only had an attic that you could get into through a little square door directly over the stairwell. One Christmas, Dad and Mother hid our Santa Claus in this attic. Marie and I found them so we really had fun from then until Christmas crawling in this attic playing with our Christmas gifts. I don't know hardly how we kept from falling and breaking our necks for it really was not an easy job getting in that old attic.

When Grandpa and Grandma lived in this house a year or two before, cousins Opal and Roy told Marie, Myrt, Cliff, and me that the upstairs was haunted and that the ghost would only walk around when there was music in the house, so we would all sit down by the piano, and Opal would play like thunder while Roy tapped a broom handle across the upstairs floor. Of course, us kids were spellbound, and I don't remember if we missed Roy from the group or not. Grandpa had an old cart with shafts *[tongues]*, I guess that is what you called them. Anyway it was a one-horse cart that we used to take each other riding on. One time Roy had been real good and took us all for a ride then came his turn, and it took Marie, Cliff, and I all to pull him so when we got going good, Cliff said, "Let's turn the shafts loose." So we did and they all flew up and dumped Roy real hard on the ground. I always felt bad about that for that was a dirty trick. Cliff had to run like crazy to get away from Roy, for he was so mad about that trick.

Opal was the best ever at making candy and popcorn balls. We kids loved those candy-making sessions. One of her specials was taffy, and she could do it to perfection. One time during one of these candy-making sessions, Marie got so excited and was dancing all around the kitchen table and someone called her Santa, and from then on for a long time everyone called her Santa. Myrt has always been called Myrt short for Myrtle. I was "Deduse." I think Carl probably started that, for so long the family called me by my double name, Mildred Ruth, and that was just too much of a mouthful for Carl so he ran it all together and it came out "Deduse." Carl was called "Buck" at home, and I really don't know exactly how that came about, but one time Aunt Ethel and her family visited with us at Seagoville and Gladys called Carl "Carmen" and we older girls called him that for a long time, then he was called "Bucky" by the younger brother and sisters. Ella Mae became "Tis" and sometimes "Titter". I suppose that was short for sister. Ray was called "Pete" and to this day we still call him that sometimes. I could not remember just how that came about, but Myrt said she thought it was something concerning a comic strip they were reading. J.B. (John) was always "Jaber." Juanita was "Puss." One time Arnold and I were there, and they had some kittens. Arnold and I wanted one of the little male cats so Juanita went out and got one for us to bring home. Arnold asked her if she was sure it was a little boy cat, and Juanita told him yes she was sure. So after we got home with our cat and called it "Tom" for a few weeks, then Arnold discovered it was a little girl cat so from then on everyone teased Juanita and called her "Puss," and our little cat was called "Pussita."

Getting back to Seagoville and Grandma Lewis, she was such a good cook, not fancy but oh so tasty and well-seasoned. She always kept a big pan of tea cakes on the top of her old icebox, and what a delight they were for all us grandkids. Do you know I can never remember going to that pan and finding it empty? I used to go spend one week with them every summer and sew for her. She would have yards of pink-and-blue-checked gingham to make cook aprons—she never went without a cook apron—and also pillowcases and hem sheets. I don't think Grandma ever went shopping much herself, especially for groceries. She would make a long grocery list of the things she wanted, and Grandpa and the boys would see to it that they were brought home to her. One of her specialties was what she called a fruitcake, but it was her good teacake dough rolled out thin and cut out the size of a plate and baked in thin layers and then she would put them together with her spiced dried apples that she had cooked and mashed real good. This cake was really delicious after it had sat overnight. Grandma would work all morning in the kitchen and cleaning house, then when the dishes were done after noon she would put on a clean apron and sit in her rocking chair all afternoon. She pieced quilts some, but I can't remember that she ever sewed much. She was real heavyset, big in the tummy but narrow in her shoulders, so she was hard to fit. I think they bought most of her clothes already made. I believe I made her a few dresses after I grew older.

Grandpa encouraged me to read, which I liked anyway, and he was always coming up with a good book for me to read while I was there. The big old Family Bible was always lying out on a table, real handy for us kids to thumb through, read and study the pictures, which were not only educational, but also entertaining. It never seemed to bother Grandpa or Grandma that we might tear a page. It was simply put there for our use. My, but how I would love having that old Bible to have kept in our family. As I've already said, Grandpa was very religious, and one book I remember him wanting me to read was *Ruth*, I think, but I don't remember the author. Anyway, it was a debate between a group of young people, Methodist and Baptist, and of course the young Baptists convinced the young Methodists over to their side.

Mother was also a bookworm, and when she saw that I dearly loved to sew, she had all the patience in the world to show me how, for she did not like to sew, even though she could. Aunt Birdie and Aunt Ethel were the seamstresses in her family, and while she taught school she would buy the material for them to sew for her. As a result I began to do the family sewing quite young in life. My childhood ambition was to become a great artist. I dearly loved to draw, and I wanted to paint, but as the family well knows there was no money to further our education after high school, so I guess I have satisfied myself with the creating of clothes. There has been a lot of satisfaction in that business for me beyond the money that I've earned. Myrt is a very good hand to sew, but Marie was like Mother as she could do it but did not like it. I think it is just great that (nieces) Karyl and Reatha were both good at it. Ella Mae and Juanita both do nice jobs with their sewing.

Along about this time I made my first cake. Dad and Mother had gone to town and left Marie, Myrt and I at home, so I suggested to them we bake a cake, and they really got excited about it. We got our fire going in the old wood cook stove, and Marie read the recipe while I measured and stirred. We got it in the oven and started our icing and when we came to where it said cook until it spins a thread, Myrt said, "Oh, I'll go get a spool of thread." Anyway, we got it finished before Dad and Mother got home, and they both showed their appreciation so much for what we had done. As I remember I don't think it was quite done. Guess we had our stove too hot. Anyway, I had to bake cakes from then on. One time I took one of the hot caps off the old cook stove and put it over by the wood box. Then Carl came along and fell on it and really burned his little arm from his elbow to his shoulder. He had such a sore arm for so long and, my, how it hurt me to see my little brother burned because I had put the hot cap in the wrong place.

Mother used to make the best homemade light bread. She had everlasting yeast that she used all the time and added to it each time she made bread. My but I can smell that bread cooking till yet. Must have been what we call sourdough bread now.

At this time we all attended church at Pleasant Grove Baptist Church. I was in the card class and sat on the front seat. I remember so well Great Uncle George Lewis led the singing and Floy Lewis (Great Uncle John's oldest daughter) played the old pump organ. Grandpa Lewis was a very good tenor singer. Great

Uncle George used to teach singing schools. One time there in church, Mother and Aunt Ione had quite a time with Myrt and Jake. One of them broke wind, and they got so tickled that Mother and Aunt Ione like never too have got them to hush and were so embarrassed by their children's behavior. Actually, I think they were as tickled as the kids were. The Church would have all day services sometimes, and everyone would bring their dinner and spread it on long lines of white tablecloths on the ground under some huge trees. That was always a great day for me. Baptism services were always held at a big tank of water in a big pasture.

The big July 4th community fish fries were also a big highlight for all us kids. Families would go to the river in wagons and have all-day picnics, and the men would catch fish with nets. There were barrels of lemonade, cakes, pies, and all the goodies. Grandma Lewis dearly loved to fish, and the boys were always good to help her get set. One time she told Dad she wanted a drink of water, so he said okay. He would find something to bring her a drink in. They were always pulling pranks on her, so he just happened to find a child's potty that he washed out real good and took her a drink. Of course, she was just horrified and everyone got a good laugh. Another time they came in with a big sack of fish and managed to let a big green bull-frog jump out at Grandma's feet. Reminds me of the time J.B. told me he had a mongoose he brought for me to see in his nicely built cage. Of course, I fell for his gag hook, line, and sinker. When he got me all set in the right spot, he eased the trap door and out jumps an old fox tail. Preston, you and Marc will remember that for you boys and your mother got as much fun out of that as your dad did. It was always amazing to me how sober you boys could be while J.B. pulled his pranks on us, never in the least giving him away.

Mother and Dad would go to Combine, a county store owned and operated by Great Uncle George and Aunt Linnie Lewis, to buy all our groceries and dry goods. They lived upstairs above the store, and we always had a good time when we went there. They had the first radio I remember; had to listen to it with earphones so only one could listen at a time. Also, we kids used to peep around in the back storehouse where they had some old wooden coffins stored. They must have been there from the late 1800s, and they always gave me such a weird feeling, but I could not keep from looking at them. Byron said they finally burned them up. Byron was Uncle George's oldest son. He and his wife Ruby operated the store up until just a few years ago.

Clarence and Alice Hitt lived across the orchard from us. Dad, Mother, Clarence and Alice had so much fun playing forty-two together at night. I tell about this now as some of the younger members of our family did not know about this, and Mother and Alice were the very best of friends.

If I remember right Grandpa and Grandma Lewis moved to Roscoe, Texas, about 1921 or 1922, and we went to visit them in the summer of 1923 and 1924 in an old Model T Ford. It took two days to make the trip from Dallas County. We spent the night by the side of the road somewhere near the Brazos River. In those days that was quite a trip. They had their crops all worked out when we arrived, but the big jumbo grasshoppers were coming out of the pasture eating the cotton around the fence rows so Marie, Myrt, and I went every morning with Cliff and Roy with wooden paddles, killing those big grasshoppers. Of course, we were all excited about coming out to West Texas as that was the farthest away from home we had ever been. Someone said we are almost to Sweetwater, and Ella Mae asked, "Will we fall in the sweet water?"

Dad and Mother decided to move to West Texas in October 1924. Dad and Mr. Will Alton, an uncle of Aunt Sue's, who was also moving his family to Roscoe, chartered a railroad car to move all our household goods and livestock, and Mr. Alton came along with the things on the freight car. Dad could not get possession of the place where we were to live until January 1st, so Uncle Clint and Aunt Annie let us stay in two rooms of their house, and we helped them pick their cotton. I can hardly imagine now what it must have been like with eleven kids, twelve years old and under, and four adults in a four-room house. There were six of us children then, and I think Uncle Clint and Aunt Annie had five at that time, and, of course, I was the oldest. [Cousin] Helen used to have mad fits if she did not get her way about everything, and she would do a mad dance. Arthur Duncan *[American tap dancer]* could probably have learned some new steps could he have witnessed one of her fits.

One night Grandpa, Dad, and all his brothers went to Roscoe to the picture show, and it kind of teed off Mother, Aunt Annie and all us kids, but I guess taking eleven kids to a show would not have been an easy job, and they probably did not have the money anyway. After they left, we all decided we would hide the old car that was left there in the yard. Neither Mother nor Aunt Annie could drive, so we pushed it way out behind the barn. We really had to push, and Mother and Aunt Annie kept yelling PUSH! PUSH! So after awhile I yelled back, "I'm pushing like HELL!" Mother and Aunt Annie just quit and sat down on the old running board of the car and laughed. Mother was just too tickled to spank me for what I said, but I guess it did relieve the tension some, and I don't remember that she even got after me for saying such a thing.

Dad and Mother had heard such stories about the terrible sandstorms of West Texas that they kept us out of school all that year. I don't think it mattered to us kids. The next year, 1926, we moved south of Roscoe on the Val Forrester place and stayed there until 1930. We went to school at Goode, a little two-teacher school, two miles from our house. We never did get to start to school until after Christmas as we had to help gather the crop, but most everyone else had to do the same thing so it wasn't so bad. Those were enjoyable years there, and we had good teachers, and they saw to it that we made up the lost time and passed our grades. We had some really good basketball games on our outside courts and programs on Friday afternoons. If the school needed money for something extra to use at school, we would have a box supper which was always fun. On one occasion we all picked cotton an afternoon or two or on Saturday to get a phonograph and records that we needed for Music Memory. I remember Dad was on the school board here at Goode for a term or two.

One of the years we lived here Dad worked at the U.S. Gypsum Mill in Sweetwater, and Marie, Myrt, and I made the crop. Dad had three teams and three one-row plows and planters, so we each had our own team. That was quite an experience, but we got the job done and even learned to set our own plows. I was always called the old cow's tail of the family for being so slow, but Dad impressed on me so much that anything worth doing was worth doing right, and if I only hoed or picked one row of cotton a day to do it right. So, I really tried to do just that. The rest of the family sure did hate to help me out when quitting time came, but they would rather *[do that]* than leave me out there all alone to finish my row. However, Dad always put my cotton on the front of the wagon because it was clean and free of trash, and they always took the sample off the front of the wagon at the gin, so maybe my slowness paid off a little. Really, I was so slow that I would even hold my team back slower than the others trying to do a good job. My planter was an old antique number with a seed box high behind my seat and a bit top-heavy. Marie and Myrt have always laughed about one time I came out to the turning row and began to turn around and my team turned a bit too short and rolled me over. They were so tickled because I said to my team, "Now turn me over."

J.B. was born June 15, 1926, and he was such a big healthy fellow with the exception of his eyes. There were several months of real worry for fear he might never see, then came that happy day when Dad held up his red Prince Albert tobacco can. As Dad moved it about in front of him, and his little eyes began to follow the tobacco can. How happy we all were to have that assurance that he did see. In fact, our cup of happiness truly ran over that day.

Juanita came along December 11, 1928. She was always such a pretty baby and, of course, petted by all of us, just the usual baby of a big family. She dearly loved to brush and fix her hair, and we all loved for her to brush our hair for she could simply put you to sleep with that good brushing. She was noted for hunting an easy way to do things. On one occasion she was sent to drive the cows home in the afternoon (Another member of the family should tell this as I was already working away from home and did not see this performance). She took the little red wagon along and tied one of the cow's tail to the tongue of the wagon, got in the wagon and had her pull her to the house. When they got to the gate, a wheel of the wagon hit the gate post and broke the switch off the cow's tail. They said she jumped out of the wagon untied that bushy tail and threw it as far as she could and was heard to say, "I didn't know it would break." (This happened while the family lived at Blackwell in 1933.) I guess Ella Mae had to milk that cow, for she tells how hard that old cow could rap you with that old stump tail.

You could only go through the ninth grade at Goode School, so Marie and I started to school at Roscoe in September 1929. I finished in 1931 and Marie in 1932. Those were really hard years, and I hardly knew how Dad and Mother managed. In the summers to help out with family expenses, Marie, Myrt, and I would hoe for some of the neighbors for one dollar a day for ten hours while Dad finished plowing out our crop. Oh, yes, and in those years there was no washing machines either, just their washboards and tubs with the big black wash pot in the backyard to heat the water. Also, the only bathtub was a No. 3 washtub and a path to the outhouse. On one occasion (perhaps a lot more, we did not know about) Ray and J.B. decided it was a lot more interesting to use the top of the outhouse rather than the inside (probably the air was a bit fresher on top). Anyway, Ray slipped off the wet top and broke his arm. I don't know if they ever used the top again or not.

Ella Mae was always getting her tongue twisted and was noted for her funny sayings. Often my job in the late afternoon was to make biscuits for supper while Mother gathered the eggs. Once I told Ella Mae to go ask Mother how much bread to make. So she ran and asked Mother, and she told her to tell me two cups of milk and a little over. So Ella Mae hurried back and told me, "Mother said to make a little two cups and all over." Then one time she came in with the seat of her black sateen bloomers torn, and Mother asked her how in the world she did that, and she said, "I was crawling through the fence, and I just stucked it up." One time at school they were studying Texas history about the fall of the Alamo, and she piped up and asked, "Did it really fall down?" Carl came home real embarrassed with Ella Mae, and she says Mother always told her that she never did get anything straight. Years later after she was married, she came to visit us and we went to church. When church was over and she shook hands with the minister, she could not think of her own name. She first said Ammons, McRorey, then Lewis, so I told the preacher she was Mrs. Whitworth. She has always said she did not know what she would have done if I had not been along to tell the preacher who she was. But she has been so much fun in the family and such a good sport about all her boo-boos. It is so good when you can laugh at your own mistakes, and she always can.

Somehow I got sidetracked by the things the younger brothers and sisters did so now I'll get back to mine and Marie's high school days. She and I worked part of the time for our room and board. The year I was a senior Dad moved north of town in the Roscoe District, and I drove the old Dodge touring car Dad had, and we all went to school at Roscoe. The next year we lived in the Brownlee School District, west of Roscoe, so Marie stayed in town, worked for her room and board and finished that spring, while the other kids all went to Brownlee. One time Marie, Myrt, and I went to Roscoe to a program and on the way home struck some loose gravel and slipped in the ditch, and it was just right for the fence post to tear the whole side off the top of the old Dodge touring car. It was a mess, but I can't remember that Dad said very much, and he still let me take the car for us to go places. Marie and Myrt would always say, "Mildred, you ask Dad if we can go for he will let us if you ask." I really think that was just an easy way out for them.

The year 1932 was very wet and seasonable, and Dad made such a good crop of everything, but things were so cheap that it didn't amount to very much. Marie had finished school in the spring, and that fall Jake, Carl, Marie, and I (Uncle Clyde, Aunt Ione and their boys lived just across the field from us) headed over a hundred ton of maize. We had a sled with a big box on it, and when we got the box full we would dump it on the ground to dry. Then Dad and Uncle Clyde came along loading it in the old truck they had and took it to Roscoe to sell at four dollars per ton. Marie and I enjoyed Carl and Jake, and even though it was a lot of work there were a lot of fond memories and good laughs. Added to that, I believe it was seventy-six bales of cotton that we made and picked that year on top of all the days and days of canning peas, beans, corn, okra, pumpkin, and pickles, but there was very little money so that is mostly what we lived on the next year. If I remember right, we also canned a beef. Dad also had a pretty good wheat crop, and the Home Demonstration agent suggested boiling the whole grain wheat for cereal, which Mother and Aunt Ione did. Chewing that stuff, it was so waxy it would nearly slip out from under your teeth, but it was not so bad after all. They also had some of the wheat ground into whole wheat flour, and the bread made out of it was fair as long as you ate it hot, but I just could not stand it cold. No one else could either. The important thing is that we all had good health and most everyone else was in the same financial bind so we could all laugh about it and share what we did have. In fact, I truly believe everyone was happier then than they are now with all their material gain.

The old house we lived in there was an old-fashioned, two-story one where you had to go through the living room (which was mine and Marie's bedroom) out on the front porch to go upstairs. The boys slept out there so it was a little inconvenient when we older girls had boyfriends to entertain, and the brothers wanted to go to bed. Of course, on a cold wet night they really would hate to go out the back door and all around the house to reach the stairs. One time J.B. bravely undressed (they slept in their long-handle underwear) and ran through the living room with his hands over his face while his little end-gate flopped open in front of Marie and her boyfriend. Later the boys solved that problem by going into the closet under the stairs and pulled a plank from behind the stairs so they could crawl through and go to bed without having to disturb those in the living room or go outside either. They were always pretty good at figuring out ways and means of getting things done for their advantage.

One Saturday night Marie and I had dates with Gus and Overton Bryant, and we went to a neighbor's to a dance. It really started raining, and just before we got to our pasture gate coming home we got stuck in the mud, and I mean stuck. It kept raining so hard that we had to sit there until daylight then walk home. My black high heel shoes had always hurt my feet, but after that walk in the mud they never did hurt any more. I decided if ever I had another pair of shoes that hurt my feet, I'd just take a long walk in the mud.

One Sunday afternoon Myrt and I wanted to go to Brownlee to visit a friend, and Myrt wanted to go horseback. Dad said okay, but told Myrt she better watch or that old mare would get away from us. Myrt had been riding her, so she thought she knew what she was doing. She got on bareback, and I climbed up behind her. Sure enough, she dropped the reins or something, and that old nag landed us in the bois d'arc tree in the front of the yard, my high heel shoes going every direction. Myrt ran over to me and said, "Get up quick before Dad sees us," but he saw it. Anyway, we walked to Brownlee, and that was my last horseback ride.

There was some kind of misunderstanding between Dad and Mr. Woodward, the owner of the place where we lived. Dad thought he had the place rented for the next year, but Mr. Woodward said no and Dad went to court with it, but of course the court ruled in favor of the landowner, and we had to move off the place. Dad rented this place at Blackwell, Texas, and we moved there in February 1933. Dad made two crops there before moving to the Busby community in Fisher County. That fall of 1933 I went to Snyder and worked for a Mrs. C.W. Popnoe, a school teacher, keeping her little girl. Jobs were so few you simply took what you could get. Anyway, what I made helped to support the family. The next year Marie was lucky and got a pretty good job with Texas Relief Commission as a case worker in Sweetwater. In a few months they began to hire some case aides, and I was lucky enough to get on. Between us we were able to kind of get Dad out of his financial bind.

Never shall I forget how much fun and pleasure Marie and I had that fall shopping and planning Christmas for the family. We made pillowcases and embroidered them at night, bought sheets, bedspreads, towels and washcloths. In fact, Mother had done without for so long that she simply needed everything you could think of and, of course, she had already done a good job of teaching us to be practical. We got clothes for all the family and some toys for the little brothers and sisters. In short we had a ball.

Myrt and I met our future husbands at Blackwell. Myrt and Bill married in the fall of 1934 just before Dad and Mother moved to Fisher County. Marie and I worked another year at Sweetwater helping the family. Mother worked so very hard with her chickens, milk and butter, helping out all she could. Dad made some good crops there and, of course, the boys, Ella Mae and Juanita were all growing up and able to take us older girls's place in the field, which they did to help Dad out. They were all taught to work just like we older girls were. My job played out in Sweetwater in the summer of 1935, and I went to work for Carlisle and Co. General Merchandise at Blackwell in July 1935.

Arnold McRorey and I married February 16, 1937, and in November of that year we lost Carl. He was injured in a football game at Colorado City. He was in high school at that time in Roby. He sustained a broken leg and died a week later. The doctor said his heart had too much strain for a sixteen-year-old boy. This was such a trying time for the family to lose someone so young and full of life and health, our first real tragedy in the family. I don't think we were really prepared to accept it, at least I know I wasn't for at that time it looked so useless to me. Mother was never well anymore after this. She lived five years after we lost Carl, but she would have a real bad sick spell every year about October and November.

I always thought Mother bottled up her grief over the loss of Carl, trying to make it easier for the rest of us. In the fall of 1941, Arnold and I persuaded Dad and Mother that it might do her good to come to our house for a while. They agreed. We four older girls, all married then, were taking turns staying one week at a time helping to take care of Mother. Arnold and I thought we could take care of her in our home and do our work at the same time. We had a lot of chickens and were milking several cows, which made it hard for Arnold to manage by himself while I was away. Also, we had such a good garden, and I did a lot of canning for us as well as some for Mother and Dad, so it did make it easier for Arnold and me. Mother said to me one day, "It seems to me you get your work done with the least effort of any one I ever saw." This again was because I was slow. She enjoyed helping me prepare the vegetables when she felt like it. She stayed five weeks and seemed to do just fine, yet she was not happy being away from Dad and the other younger children—

Ray, J.B., and Juanita—at home. As for me, I shall always treasure those five weeks I had with Mother. Her two sisters, Aunt Ethel and Aunt Birdie, came and spent one week with her while she was at our house, and they enjoyed each other so very much. I am so glad as that was her last time to get to visit with her sisters.

Aunt Birdie was a bookworm, too, and when she found out that I had not read *St. Elmo*, she sent her book to me to read after she went home. I enjoyed it so very much. They simply kept Mother in stitches all week talking about their childhood and telling her little funny jokes. Billie Nell was her only grandchild then, and Myrt would bring her lots in the afternoon, and Mother really enjoyed her little granddaughter. Dad, the boys, and Juanita would come on weekends, which helped her lots, but she still wanted to go home, and I can understand that so well. She went home the last of October, took real sick again in November, and was never able to be up again. We lost her in September 1942, only fifty-six years of age and that seems so young to me now.

Dad truly lost his prop when he lost her. I don't believe Dad had ever realized just how much he depended on her for everything, us children too for that matter, for even to this day there are things I'd like to talk to her about. She did her job well with her family and, personally, I'm truly proud of all my brothers and sisters for the teachings of our parents have more than proved themselves to me in the good moral Christian citizens they have all turned out to be. I do not make this statement out of vanity, but real humble pride and joy at having had the pleasure and opportunity of being a member of this family. I'm just as proud of the girls that Ray and J.B. married. They are both good Christian girls and have made such admirable wives and mothers that fit into our family perfectly, just two more lovable sisters. The brothers-in-law also have fit into the family so well and the nieces and nephews, how mother would have enjoyed all of them which makes me realize again how much our family has been blessed all these years and how much we really have to be thankful for.

Ray had gone into defense work in Dallas before mother passed away and, of course, went on into the service of his country during World War II. He made the Normandy Invasion and saw a lot of combat duty in Europe. The Lord blessed us again in keeping him safe, and I think it was after he got home from the war that I finally got my answer as to why Carl was taken like he was, for I came to realize all of a sudden just how much he and all of us may have been spared, and I was able at last to thank God for it. Ray was always so good to write home and we each shared his letters. When he was at Aachen, Germany he changed Arnold's initials in our address on his letters to let us know where he was. He could not tell us as his letters were censored, and, of course, we had to get several letters before we could figure it out. J.B. was a bit too young for World War II, but he did his tour of duty for his country as a Merchant Marine. I know it broadened his education for he got to visit many places. I think most of us girls still have some gifts that he would send from various places. I have a butterfly pin that he sent me from Thessalonica.

It looked like for some time that Arnold would have to enter the war also. He was in class I-A and had passed his first physical. He managed to get a three-month deferment to gather our crop. We lived on his grandfather McRorey's home place and got things shaped up so I could manage while he was gone. During that time he had his thirty-eighth birthday, and they at once re-classified him to III-A as they did not take men that old unless worse came to worse, so Arnold did not have to go.

Dad married again about a year after Mother passed away and needless to say home was never the same again. This was a very difficult time for J.B. and Juanita, as they were the only two at home. Dad still needed Mother's counseling. He and Beulah lived together for twelve years, then were divorced. After that Dad lived with the boys and their families for a while, which I know was not easy for them. He then married Maudie, and she lived six years. They were living at Weatherford when she passed away, and Dad was working as a custodian at the school. He stayed on alone there until he married Alice and by this time Dad was on up in his seventies. I never did think Dad was ever happy with any of the three women he married for none of them ever quite reached Mother's standards, although they were all nice women, yet I'm frank to admit Dad was too young to live alone after he lost Mother.

Dad and Alice had planned when they reached the point where they could no longer look after each other that he would come back to Sweetwater. They went to Seagoville to live after they married and, of course, all her children lived there. Dad kept being under the weather and in and out of the hospital there so in January of 1972 he came back to Sweetwater and went into the rest home of his own accord. That was such a difficult time for all of us as he began to have light strokes that affected his speech. He got to where he could not speak a word we could understand which made it so hard not only for us but for him also as he wanted to tell us things and we simply could not understand him. It was so hard to walk off and leave him there, but I had to console myself that he was being cared for so much better than any of us could have done in our homes. I know that all the other members of the family felt the same way. Dad died with so much dignity. He did not want to misput any of us, and even the nurses said he was such a good patient. Bill, Myrt, Marie, Ella Mae, and I were all with him when he passed away, and Jurdene had only been gone a few minutes. Myrt and I had been to see him the day before, and he was asleep, so we did not try to arouse him, yet we thought he did not look exactly right, but the nurse assured us he was just sleeping. The next morning when Marie, Ella Mae, and Jurdene went to see him, they knew for sure all was not well and called us. We went as quickly as we could, and he was gone by mid-afternoon April 5, 1972, and we laid him to rest by the side of Mother and Carl in the Sweetwater Cemetery. In all honesty, I would have to say there was a feeling of relief at seeing him look so peaceful and at rest at last, even though it is always hard to say goodbye for a time, but at the same time look forward to the eternal reunion.

As a family we were very poor in material wealth, but very wealthy in the things that really count, for we never lacked for love, understanding and family fun. Dad was no manager as I've already said but he would have given any of us the very shirt off his back or the last dollar he had if he thought we needed it.

When we girls began to have dates I remember so well Dad telling us, "Your mother and I have tried to raise you in the right way, and I don't think you will let us down." So he let us know he trusted us, and I'm sure that made us much more careful than we might have been under different circumstances, for it would have been real hard to have betrayed their trust in us.

There may be some other things I could have written about, but I've told this as near as I could the way I remember and what impressed me the most. So I would say to my family, "Due to the deep love and concern that God has shown us, then I hope we shall always practice tender-hearted mercy and kindness to others and accept the advice Paul gave in Colossians 3:14-15: 'Most of all, let love guide your life, for them the whole church will stay together in perfect harmony. Let the peace of heart which comes from Christ be always present in your hearts and lives, for this is your responsibility and privilege as members of his body. And always be thankful'."

In Loving Memory
Mildred Ruth Lewis McRorey
Blackwell, Texas
1974

CHAPTER FOUR

Grace Marie Lewis Ammons

After reading the memoirs of Mildred, Ella Mae, Myrt and Billie Nell, I feel they have covered the story of our lives completely. Yet as I read their episodes, they bring to mind a number of things. I want to say, as each of them has, that our childhood and teen years in a family of ten were happy ones and rich in every way except material possessions. But you know I'm afraid people today are striving toward material things and have kinda lost sight of or don't have time for close family relations.

Looking back, it's hard to realize that my life span has covered the days of the horse and buggy (and wagon), Model T, Cadillac, airplane, atomic power, jets, *[outer]* space and entering the solar age. What more can the next forty years bring?

I was born in Plano, Texas, but have few memories of that time for we moved to Seagoville before Myrt was born, and I was just past two years old when she came along. I do remember three houses we lived in at Seagoville, and they were all in a straight line, probably not far apart, but to a small child it seemed like a long way. Mildred told about the cyclone blowing our house away. I remember following with enthusiasm the building of the new house, three rooms with a porch across the front and painted red. That spring was a stormy one, and I remember one night in the new house lightning struck close by and came in on the telephone line. Mother had a straight pin in her mouth, and it melted and just left the print of a pin on her tongue. We made many trips to the neighbor's storm cellar before Daddy got one ready.

That fall Mother and Daddy had a time picking cotton. A whirlwind would come along and scare Mildred, Myrt and me, and just about the time they would get us settled down and get back to their sack, here would come another whirlwind. Mildred told about the Trinity River getting out of its banks and us leaving our home. I, too, will never forget our boat ride back home with Uncle George. The fence posts were still under water, and I remember him hitting one of them and nearly dumping us. We had some fun taking a No. 2 tub for a boat and rowing around in the pasture as the water receded. Another experience was taking lunch to Daddy and some of his distant cousins who worked with Daddy for a year or two when they worked land across the slough. There was a girl older than Mildred, Myrt and me, and we would wade in the water while the men ate. One day I went too far out and got in water over my head. I went under two or three times and can remember thinking I was drowning and wouldn't see my family anymore when this older girl caught my dress tail and pulled me back to shallow water. I've always been afraid of water.

I started to school at Rains Hall, a three-teacher school, and I think my first teacher was a Mrs. Roach. My first experience with snuff was on the way home from school one afternoon when an older girl gave me some. I made the mistake of breathing in as I put it in my mouth, and I thought I would strangle. Needless to say, I had no desire to try that again.

We went to church at Pleasant Grove Baptist Church, and I would guess it was about four miles distance. My mental picture of Mother was singing in the choir, and she wore what to me was the prettiest white long sleeve blouse, brown skirt, and a perky little pill box hat over her long hair. She was beautiful, as was her character. She did love life, her family and all people. Ralph said mother could talk to you on any subject. She loved to read and kept up on what was happening. How she would have enjoyed knowing all her grandchildren and their families. Billie Nell was only four and Reatha about six months old when Mother died.

Mother called me to her bedside one afternoon and told me that she was converted and joined the First Christian Church when she was fifteen years old; that she had always intended to join the Baptist Church with Daddy, but somehow was never quite able to do it. I told her that I was just as happy with her being in the First Christian Church as in the Baptist and her reply was, "You don't know how happy it makes me to hear you say that." She talked on awhile and said how much she would love to see her grandchildren grow up. We have missed her so much.

There was a time before Carl Preston was born that Mother's health was not good, and we girls went to a Church of Christ church with the Mathis family in a wagon. They had girls our ages, and we used to trade out spending the night. Mildred would stay with Cleo, and Altie would come with me and vice versa. We also used to look forward to one night during the school year asking our teacher home with us.

As Mildred and Ella Mae said, our Christmases were meager as far as gifts go, but how we did enjoy them. After Christmas one year, Mother found some storybooks that Santa forgot to put out. They were between her mattress and feather bed! Then one year Santa brought Carl a bucking mule hooked to a cart. He was sitting on Mother's lap while Daddy wound the spring and put the toy on the floor. Carl hollered, "Whoa," and jumped out of Mother's lap onto the toy, and it never bucked any more.

Grandpa and Grandma Lewis moved to Seagoville and bought a grocery store. That spring Roy and Cliff came out and hoed for Daddy, and they always brought a supply of candy and chewing gum, a real treat for us, but not too good for Grandpa's grocery business. I remember months later Daddy finding a pear that Roy had laid up over the door sill to ripen. It was very mellow! A treat in the fall was to ride a bale of cotton to the gin with Daddy on Saturday and get a quarter to spend. We came home with red soda pop and candy all over us, but enjoyed every minute of it. I'm sure Mother got a much-needed rest while we were gone.

Mildred, Myrt and I had a way of hiding out after meals and played till we heard that certain tone in Mother's voice that we knew meant it was time to go do the dishes. J.B. had his own special way of preparing Mother for his request, and I think it worked a lot of the time. Possibly he had a special little corner of their hearts for when he was born, the doctor told Mother and Daddy that he would never see. He was a large baby and through difficult birth his eyes were bloodshot, and the doctor really thought he would be blind. As Mildred has already told, what a day of rejoicing when Daddy got J.B. to follow the movement of his red Prince Albert tobacco can.

Mother and Daddy had a way of discussing the family finances at the table and made us feel we had a part in it. We were always concerned when our prospects for a crop were not good. In fact, I can't remember many times we older girls asking for money for we usually knew Daddy didn't have it to spare. I had my first pair of white shoes after I got out of high school. They were linen or canvas with a little eyelet flower embroidered on the toe, and I think they cost ninety-eight cents, but I was proud of them for they were summer shoes.

One thing I remember about the trip to West Texas to visit Grandpa and Grandma Lewis in 1923 was the mountains. But first thing was our accident in Dallas. A young boy was driving his grandfather's car (looked like a Cadillac to us) and ran into our Model T. The old man was so sure our car was not hurt and seemed to want us to get on our way before the police came. Daddy looked the car over and couldn't see anything wrong so we left. As soon as we drove off, he could hardly steer the car. Of course, the old fellow and boy had already driven off so Daddy stopped first chance and found the axle was bent. That took awhile *[to fix]* at a blacksmith shop, as I remember. We stopped at Gordon, Texas, late in the afternoon to visit a brother of Aunt Ione Lewis's father, Mr. Hitt. It seemed to me that we were completely surrounded and pinned in by those huge mountains. I would have given most anything I had to have been back to the safety of our home in Seagoville. I just couldn't see how we would ever get out of that big old hole we were in, but we did. We drove in to Grandpa's about 5 p.m. the next day after spending the night by the side of the road. It seemed so cool in West Texas, and I remember after getting back home at midday it just seemed there was not enough air to breathe.

Ray was born that following November 13th and the next summer we almost lost him with intestinal flu. Aunt Stella (Dad's sister) was a registered nurse, and she came to wait on him. I remember after he made a change for the better how excited and thrilled we were when he reached that small hand up for his bottle of milk the first time. He had to learn to crawl again and was some bit over a year old when he began to walk.

By that time we had moved to West Texas, and I think Mildred and Myrt have told all about that. Even though we did not go to school that first year at Wastella, we had an enjoyable time. Mother and Daddy let us order a number of books from Sears Roebuck that Christmas, and some I remember were *English Orphans, Lena Rivers*, and *Black Beauty*. My how we enjoyed reading, just living the story as we read and crying about as much as we read. Mildred may still have some of those books. The pasture where our house stood was a regular prairie dog town, and we spent a lot of time watching them.

That fall we moved south of Roscoe to the Forrester place and started to school at Goode, a two-teacher school. Those were good years, and we enjoyed playing basketball (on a rough outside court) and softball. We walked two miles, but met other kids after a mile. It was not bad until a sandstorm would catch us. It was here that Mildred, Myrt and I learned to farm. We each had our team and equipment, which consisted of a one row planter and cultivator. Daddy was a good teacher and very patient with us. He could chop the neatest, most uniform row of cotton I ever saw and tried to teach us the same. It was great to come to a nice long skip that Daddy had hoed to help us keep up with him. That skip just seemed to say, "I love you, come on up."

Mildred has told you about her team, a pair of big mares named "Dutch" and "Dunny." I don't remember that mine and Myrt's had names. I usually got the more spirited teams, and one day we were about to finish plowing. In fact I was plowing the fence row when Carl came to the field and wanted to ride. I stopped and put him in the seat of my cultivator, and I walked behind. A sweep caught on something and tripped. I reached down to lift the plow, and when I released it, caught my finger. Dad was hoeing nearby and Mildred had the wrenches on her plow so I told Carl to hold the reins tight, and I called to Dad as calmly as I could. He quickly came by Mildred and got a wrench to free my finger. The end of it was as flat as a pancake, and Dr. Young said the bone was broken up, but there was nothing to do and that it would be alright; sure enough, it was. Another time one of my animals had the colic, I guess, and decided to lay down and roll. I was scared but didn't know what to do and did nothing. He rolled over too close to the other animal, and he stepped on his belly. With a bellow, which did about scare me out of my wits, he got up and started to pull and we continued plowing. I also plowed some at Blackwell with a little Spanish mare that I was scared of.

Mother and Daddy worked together in disciplining we kids. Any time Daddy heard mother tell us to do something and we hesitated a bit, Dad would say "You heard what your mother said," and we knew that meant business. They told us when we were old enough to get out without them that they expected us to conduct ourselves in a manner they would be proud of. Not that we always did that, but it was something we didn't forget.

One summer we went to a Baptist revival in Roscoe. We had gone there some with Roy and Cliff and during that revival Mildred and I were converted and joined the church. I remember the baptizing was in a creek out from Roscoe, and Mildred drove the old Dodge. It rained before we left, and the road—just a trail through the pasture—got wet and slick. Mildred was having problems sliding, so Clifton pulled up behind us and with his bumper against ours pushed us up the incline. The last day of school one year, Daddy let Mildred take the car. We came to other kids walking and when Mildred began to stop, she says, "Whoa." She had plowed more than she had driven a car.

Like Ella Mae I liked to play ball of any kind. I wanted to play basketball when I started to Roscoe, but for some reason, I didn't start workouts when the others did to gradually get used to the exercise. We were still playing on an outside court, and it was cold the first night we played. I didn't start until later in the game, and I was so sore I thought to my soul I would not be able to get moving. When we moved to Blackwell, we went to school one night to a basketball game. The outsiders were playing the school team and somehow I got in on the outside team. We were in the dressing room after the game and the girl's coach came in. I heard him ask who that girl playing forward was that was so rough! Turned out it was me, and he came out to the house the next week and asked me to come to school and play on the team. I told him I had already graduated, and he said they did not have any interscholastic rules for girls' basketball. So I worked in his office some and took one or two courses and played till the season was over.

I was never blessed with a talent for sewing. One day I came home, and Myrt had made a beautiful blue-and-white-striped seersucker dress. How I did envy her and several times she let me wear that dress. My first experience with sewing was a pair of pajamas. In sewing up the pants, I came with a sort of skirt and could not figure out how I had gone wrong. Mother came in and took one look, got so tickled and said, "If you can't figure that out, I'm not going to tell you." I never did get a whole lot better and have made the remark that I had nearly rather "streak" than sew.

My first job was with the Texas Relief Commission in 1934. I'll always be grateful to Bob Jordan, who was commissioner at Blackwell, for getting me the job. Mother and Daddy had gone to Busby that day to see the place that was to be our next home. Mr. Jordan took me to Busby to get their permission to take the job, and I went to work the following Monday. I stayed with Uncle George and Aunt Sue, and I think I paid them $2 or $3 a week for room and board. I needed a car with my job so Daddy came up, and we bought a Model A, about a 1928 model. It wasn't long till Mildred also got a job with the Relief Commission, and she stayed with Hassie Price and her mother. We enjoyed work and doing things together.

Mildred's job did not require a car so that Christmas, as she told you, we loaded that old Model A with packages and headed for Blackwell. We didn't have any problems deciding what to get for anyone because everyone could use anything! I mean that literally. Today our children would chuckle at what we bought, but even little kitchen items as well as the pillowcases, sheets, bedspread, towels, etc., that Mildred mentioned for Mother were needed. I don't remember if we got her any clothes, but we got Dad some overalls; toys and, I think, maybe some clothes for the kids. We have had some wonderful Christmases since, but none will ever surpass that one for Mildred and me. The first of that year, the family moved to Busby and again, Mildred and I enjoyed buying things for the house. Myrt and Bill McRorey had married and had their home at Blackwell.

That's *[the Busby dwelling]* the first Mother and Daddy had had a house with enough room to have a living room, so Mildred and I furnished that. We bought a rose-colored linoleum square, a velour couch with some rose in it, a chair to match, a little table, lace panels and rose side drapes for the windows and a coal heater that was prettier than the one we used in the kitchen. We were proud of that room, and so were Mother and Daddy. Later that year, 1935, the Texas Relief Commission changed as all government programs do, and I moved to Big Spring to work in the district office. My boss had a sister living there, and I stayed with her and her husband (Mr. and Mrs. C.D. Herring). Mildred went to Blackwell and worked for Mr. Carlisle in his dry goods department. My job lasted about a year and then folded. Mr. Grover Dean, who had been my boss, his sister and I then bought a small grocery store there in the fall of 1936, and I had my one third of it clear by November 1937.

In November of 1937 tragedy struck our family. Carl was injured playing football and died on Thanksgiving Day. That was a shock to the whole family, but especially to Mother, who was having health problems. Her health continued to decline and early in 1938 she was in the hospital for several days. I decided it was best for me to come home to stay so I offered my part in the store to Mr. and Mrs. Herring with the understanding they could pay for it as they could, which they did.

Mother and I had a mother-and-daughter sharing-time while she was in the hospital, and she knew I was not happy with my situation. She told me that there was a young man in the community that she wished I could meet, and she thought he was a very nice person. I went to Liberty Baptist Church one Sunday night with Ella Mae, Ray and J.B. After church was over the young people were all outside, and I was introduced to several.

Among them was Ralph Ammons, and I remembered what Mother had told me earlier. I was real pleased when he asked me for a date and really pleased when he continued to come to see me.

He went to college in Lubbock that summer, and then in the fall he was hired to teach school at Capitola, a three-teacher school just west of the Busby community. At the end of that school year on May 20, 1939, we were married. Arlie McDaniels was pastor of the Liberty church and also the El Paso Baptist Church, so we arranged to meet him at Mr. and Mrs. Homer Elam's in the El Paso community. He was to have services at El Paso that Sunday, and he performed our ceremony that Saturday night. We came back to Mother and Daddy's on Sunday for lunch and to Ralph's parents that night.

Monday morning we left for Los Angeles, California, to spend the summer with Marvin and Elsie (Ralph's sister). We took Doris Lister with us, and she and Mark Etter were married, which consummated a courtship begun at Busby while Mark was working at the gin and Doris was teaching school. Bless Marvin and Elsie, they moved out of their bedroom to the living room so the two newlywed couples could have the bedrooms. I don't think we really knew how to appreciate the sacrifice they made for us—they made us feel so welcome. Mark had a permanent job, and Ralph worked at an icehouse until time for school to start, and then we came back to Texas.

It was a custom to chivaree newlyweds, but we left for California too soon so when we got back they were pretty determined to get us. One Sunday night after church Mother knew the plans, so she suggested I change from my housecoat, and we got suspicious. We went to Floyd and Scena Woods, hid the car and went to bed (they were not at home). Someone brought Ernest Ammons and Ray and let them out some distance from the house to keep us at home. Well, Mother felt sorry for them so she hinted at where they might find us. Ralph and I had dozed off to sleep when here everyone came. They were pretty rough on Ralph, dragged him through a patch of grass burrs, and we picked out stickers for weeks. After that they gave us a nice shower. Mother and Daddy let us have a bedroom and a back shed room that we fixed up for a kitchen.

That let me stay with Mother, and Ralph drove back and forth to Capitola. The next summer we spent in Lubbock for Ralph to go to school. Dorothy was also in college so she and another teacher shared an apartment with us. After the next school year we went back to California for the summer. Mark and Doris had moved into their own apartment, and we stayed with Marvin and Elsie again.

Let me back up a bit: Mother got real sick and was in the hospital when we planned to leave so Ralph left me to help care for Mother and come on to California when I could. I don't remember how long it was before I caught an All-American bus for a reunion with my husband—was I excited? The bus broke down just outside Phoenix, Arizona, in the middle of the night, and we were delayed several hours. I sent Ralph a telegram from Phoenix with a new arrival time. We did get in, and Ralph, Marvin and Elsie were there to meet me. Surely was good to see them waiting when the bus stopped—another enjoyable summer. When we got back to Texas, we were expecting our first child. We lived that year in one room of the Capitola school building. We divided one big room into three with cotton sacking. This gave us a living bedroom, bedroom and kitchen. It left a lot to be desired, but it also had some good points.

We were at Mother and Daddy's December 7th when news of the Pearl Harbor attack came over the radio. That was a solemn evening. I went to bed early, rather depressed as Ralph was a very ripe age for the draft. He came in soon after and gave me a good talking [to], saying he had more to fight for and defend than any of the single men. As days passed and we talked and heard more newscasts, Ralph decided to go talk to the draft board. They pretty well assured him he would be called by the time school was out in May. He definitely preferred the air force and had a desire to fly. After checking qualifications for a pilot, he found that twenty-seven years was the limit and he would be twenty-seven March 3rd. I reasoned that if he definitely wanted to fly, it would be better to volunteer a few months early rather than to be drafted into the regular army. He began the procedure to get in pilot training, and I just prayed that if it was God's will he be a pilot that he would be accepted, and if it weren't something would happen to show him otherwise. With that, I gained some peace about it all.

Ralph left Sweetwater by bus March 22nd for San Antonio and primary training at Randolph Field. Ethel (Johnnie's wife) had told Ralph that she would go to the hospital and stay with me when our baby was born. On an April evening at 10:30 p.m. Reatha Myrl was born. Ethel sent a telegram to Ralph, and he got a weekend pass to come home. He got to Sweetwater and to the hospital at 2 a.m. Sunday morning. The nurse was bringing the babies in for their two o'clock feeding, and she let Ralph stay in the room. When the nurse came back she took Reatha and handed her to Ralph and said, "Would you like to hold her?" Needless to say we were both shocked, but pleased. The nurse did not come back for her for maybe ten or fifteen minutes. A lady who knew the Ammons family had also had a baby and was awake when Ralph came to my room. She said she heard me holler, and knew Ralph had come in. He had to catch a bus back Sunday afternoon so it was a short visit, but we treasured it.

Reatha and I went to the Ammons' *[place]* from the hospital and stayed some time, then we went back to Mother and Daddy's as Mother was in bed most of the time. Ralph went from Randolph Field to Sikeston, Missouri, for basic training and then back to Kelly Field, San Antonio, for advanced training and his commission as pilot. He came by Roby from Sikeston to Kelly Field, and then Reatha and I visited him for one week in San Antonio.

Mother grew steadily worse and had several strokes before she died on September 9th. I sent Ralph a telegram, but had no idea whether or not he could come. I had given up, and we were getting in the cars to go to the church when I saw a cloud of dust way down the road. Somehow I just knew that was Ralph, so we waited a few minutes and sure enough it was. He had had a time locating his commanding officer to get permission to come, but he got to stay through the weekend which seemed like a good while at first, but it passed all too quickly. Reatha and I stayed with Daddy, J.B. and Juanita until November when Ralph graduated. In the meantime, Joe and Ella Mae had moved back from Coleman, and Joe was going to farm with Daddy. Reatha was the apple of all our eyes, and I remember J.B. making a wagon out of an apple box and some wheels off an old wagon. I guess he pulled her several miles in it, much to her delight. We have a picture of them and the wagon.

Ralph was assigned to the bombardier school at Concho Field in San Angelo, and we stayed there until January 1945. Oh, how we enjoyed those years—close enough to come home and our folks to come visit us. Karyl was born in May of 1944 in San Angelo. I believe J.B. had come to see us, and I went to the hospital that night. It worked out good for us for he stayed with Reatha while Ralph was with me. Then the next day Ralph took Reatha to Joe and Ella Mae's to stay until we got home. Reatha cried a lot when she was small, so Karyl seemed like a real good baby. I do remember one night soon after we got home from the hospital Karyl woke up and began to cry. Ralph and I were going to wait awhile and see if she would not go back to sleep, but Reatha woke up, and pretty soon she says, "Mommy, Daddy, dat baby's crying." We tried to ignore her, too, but she got a little louder, and we decided we had better feed Karyl.

Karyl was only two weeks old when Mrs. Ammons died. I wanted to come with Ralph so bad. He suggested we check with the doctor, but I was afraid he would say no. I promised Ralph I would take care, and he gave in. I made it fine for his family took care of the girls as well as me. By that time Marvin and Elsie had moved back to Busby from California.

Ralph had two brothers in service at this time—Johnnie in the navy and Ernest in the air force as a pilot. Dorothy's husband, Jess Hall, was in the army and Loy Neeper, soon to be Arlene's husband, was in the air force. My brother Ray was with the army in the European Theater, and J.B. was soon to join the Merchant Marines.

Ralph and Johnnie bought a duplex in Sweetwater for Ethel and me and our five girls to wait out the war. Ethel and her girls were living there, and in January 1945, Ralph moved us there and left for B-17 training in Florida. Before we left San Angelo, we began to notice one of Karyl's feet didn't look right when she would stand on it. Ralph asked me to have it checked when we moved back to Sweetwater. I did and Dr. Rosebrough suggested I take her to Scottish Rite Hospital in Dallas. We had to go through the Masonic Lodge so he arranged for Mr. Cliff Boswell to make application for her. Mr. Boswell came to the house and visited awhile and explained that if they needed to do anything that would require hospitalizing Karyl that I would have to leave her and could only visit rarely. If I was not willing to do that, he need not fill out the application—my, my what a bombshell! I studied a minute, and then I believe God spoke through me for my reply was, "I have no choice, if her foot needs that much correction, I'll have to leave her." He began filling out the application.

I shall never forget that trip. Ray's wife, Maxine, was living in Dallas and working close to the depot. I was to call her when the train arrived. I was trying to get our suitcase, my purse and Karyl ready to get off when a soldier walked up and took the suitcase and asked where I was going. I told him I would call my sister-in-law from the depot so he took Karyl, set her on a counter and waited with her till I called Maxine. You know God really takes care of His people! Ruby, Maxine's sister, was not working and bless her heart she just took us under her wing, went to the hospital and stayed with us. They examined Karyl every way you could think of, and I had no idea what they were finding. When the doctor began telling me what I was to do, I asked, "Do you mean I can take her home?" He said yes and that's when I nearly lost control. Again God had His hand on us. Karyl wore a bar screwed to her shoes to pull her foot in place for three months day and night then at night for six months. After that it was high top corrective shoes for several years. She was so excited to get her first pair of red sandals and go barefoot in the summer. We took her back periodically to be checked, and Joe was so good to let Ella Mae go with us. In fact, I depended on Ella Mae and Joe, as well as Ralph's family, for so many things while Ralph was gone.

J.B. stayed with us awhile until he joined the Merchant Marines. He came home one time after having an appendicitis attack on board ship. He and the girls and I drove to Cliff and Gladys' that afternoon and night, then Gladys and Melba Hope went with us to take him to the Galveston hospital for surgery. They admitted him right after lunch so we left to come back that night, thinking his surgery would be the next morning. When we got back J.B. had had his surgery and was sitting up in bed! I think he was in the hospital only three or four days and then drove our car back to Cliff's.

When Ralph left Florida he came by Sweetwater in July and took the girls and me to Montgomery, Alabama, where he was to train in the B-29 airplane. We enjoyed being a family again until December when Ralph went overseas and us back to the duplex. It was a long year but again we were blessed to have both Ralph's and my family close by. Loy Neeper came home from overseas, and he and Arlene were married. They moved to San Angelo just as Ralph and I were leaving. I believe they stayed there until he was discharged.

When Johnnie came home Ethel and her girls moved out of the duplex, and we moved to her side as it was larger. The girls and I wrote to Ralph nearly every day, and they got a bang out of scribbling, then coming to have me read what they wrote. One day I found scribbling all over the wall by their bed and asked who did it. Karyl confessed, and I gave her a good spanking, then asked what in the world she was doing. She said, "I was writing Daddy." That was one paddling I would like to have recalled! We had one Christmas without Ralph. We sent his gifts, but learned later that a mail plane crashed. He never did get the package so I guess it was on that plane. One day our phone rang, and the operator said at a certain time the next day we would get a call from Ralph so plan to be by the phone. We were so sure he would be telling us he was on his way home, but he had flown to Tokyo, Japan, and got a chance to call. He was not coming home. It was good to talk to him, but disappointing in that it was a setup where he would talk a little and then we'd talk. I don't know if the girls ever heard his voice or not. Ralph did get home in March 1947. I believe he was the last one in our families to be discharged. Ray came home [earlier], and he and Maxine drove to Alabama to see us, a visit we enjoyed so much.

Ralph came home by boat to California, flew to Amarillo and by train on to Sweetwater. Ernest had been discharged and married Margaret Klingler. They were living in Lubbock for Ernest to go back to Texas Tech, and when Ralph came through Lubbock, they came on to Sweetwater with him. Needless to say, how excited we were. I was so afraid the girls would not recognize their daddy, but they did. Karyl was a little shy, but while we were at the supper table she got out of her chair and walked around behind Ralph letting her arm slide around his chair until she could look up at him. He took her on his lap, and they made friends right away.

We moved from the duplex to the Ammons home place in August and in the fall Ralph bought a small farm just east of Mr. Ammons's place. I remember Uncle Henry Ammons and Mr. Herman Graves built a cabinet in our kitchen that I thought was really something. I must tell about the rat episode: The Dooley family moved out as we moved in, and they swore they had not seen a rat on the place. Well, we found that rats had completely undermined the cow shed and barn. I never saw so many of the varmints. Ralph had a .22 rifle that he killed a lot of them with. Then when he was at work (he had taken a job at Jack McCain Motor Co. in Roby), I would stand at the window over the kitchen sink and shoot them as they climbed the water tank to drink. I got to be a pretty good shot. One Sunday afternoon Glendol Ammons and Howard Whitworth brought their little rat terrier dogs and their shotguns up and pretty well cleaned them out. I think Howard got a few buckshot in his leg, but they had fun, and we went out of the rat business.

This is where we had our first garden, a cow and pigs. In the spring we got a hundred little chickens. They came before we had a place ready, and we made the mistake of putting them in the cellar. They took pneumonia from the dampness and we lost about half of them. That kinda dampened my enthusiasm for raising chickens.

It was while we lived here that John Michael was born in October of 1949, an eight pound, nine ounce boy. We were two proud parents! The girls were just as proud of their baby brother. While I was in the hospital Ralph pointed to a sunflower patch out my west window and said that it was the site of our new home to be started around the first of the year.

On Sunday, January 1, 1950, the children and I were at church at Longworth. Ralph had to work at the Ford house taking inventory. When church was over, Johnnie was there to tell us that Ralph was in an accident at work and was burned. We came to the hospital, and it was somewhat of a shock to see Ralph's face, hands and one leg. His hair was singed and his face dark and beginning to swell. He was in the hospital through January and February with two weeks of that in Harris Hospital in Fort Worth for skin grafts on his leg. Johnnie and Ethel kept the three kids with Mike being only three months old. We had to put Mike on a bottle when we went to Fort Worth, and then the girls had the measles while we were gone. Poor Ethel really had her hands full. We'll be forever grateful for her and Johnnie. Marvin and Elsie were building a house in Roby, so Elsie helped Ethel some. That was a long two weeks in Fort Worth, and Ralph tells that when we started home the closer we got to Roby the faster I drove. I was anxious to get back to Roby and my family. Ralph went back to the Roby hospital for another week.

The day we left for Fort Worth our new house was begun. We moved in in June, and we are still enjoying it. We have added the garage to the house for a den, which gives us a lot more room. Ralph left McCain Motor, and we went into our own business—a flower shop and a picture and music studio. This was the beginning of the years of drought, and Ralph soon gave up the picture and music studio to run a filling station while I kept the flower shop. From the filling station Ralph went to the Ford House in Snyder as a mechanic. In 1954 we bought into Roby Hydro as partner with Preston Campbell and have sold butane, propane and diesel since.

Our children have all married and we now have six grandchildren—five girls and one boy. The fellow who said, "You haven't lived until you've been a grandparent" knew what he was talking about. Ralph had one sister, and I have two who did not have children, but I think they all loved and are loved by all our children and grandchildren so that they can agree with us on the above quotation. Our children lost their aunt Elsie a year ago this month and I feel that was more like giving up a grandmother than an aunt. Elsie filled that role in their lives for they never knew Ralph's mother.

It has been my pleasure to write these memories, and my prayer is that each of us will love and serve our Lord and be ready for that great reunion beyond this life.

God Bless Each One,
Grace Marie Lewis Ammons
Roby, Texas
1979

CHAPTER FIVE

Edna Myrtle "Myrt" Lewis McRorey

Having read and enjoyed so thoroughly the memories written by Mildred, Ella Mae, J.B., and my daughter, Billie Nell, I felt that I wanted to write some of the things that impressed me. Mine will be more brief since they have told things that I will not repeat.

I would like to say in the beginning that I am very grateful for my family. When I recall our growing up together, it's with joy. I have no regrets. We have always been a very close family, for which I'm thankful, with a good mother and daddy, five sisters and three brothers that couldn't be beat. No, we did not have a lot of worldly possessions, but how well we learned that true values did not consist of worldly things.

I was born December 20, 1915, at Seagoville, Texas, and lived the first eight years of my life there. My first and second years of school were at the country school of Rains Hall. These years are a bit hazy to me. I remember walking to and from school with the neighbor kids, and I remember pulling off my shoe and throwing it at one of the Mathis girls for teasing me about her brother. We picked wild violets along the road.

My first memory of Sunday School was at a little country church there. I was in what they called the "Card Class." I thought I was quite dressed up to go to Sunday School in a green taffeta dress with black velvet bows that my mother had made me from one of Aunt Stella's (whom I was named after; her name was Stella Myrtle). She was a nurse and would give Mother her discards to make us children's clothes. I had a pair of black satin T-strap shoes that Mama had ordered from Sears. She ordered patent and wanted to send the satin ones back, but I cried her out of it. I thought they looked cute with my taffeta dress. It was fun to sit in the back of the wagon and swing your feet, if you were lucky enough to beat the others to that choice seat. There were other choice seats so that there was always a constant warfare going on for them. One was what we kids called "the first," which was at the end of the bench, next to the head of the table where our daddy ate. Another that we bickered over was when we got a Model T car, to sit in the back next to the doors and hold onto a rod that supported the top. Ella Mae tells that choice seats for her and Ray were buckets on the floorboard.

I was young, but I remember the work I had to help do, pick cotton, shuck corn, feed the pigs and horses, carry in wood winter and summer for we cooked on a wood stove, dozens of evening chores that modern kids know nothing about. But it wasn't all bad, to sit in the trough and eat peanuts with the horses was fun, as long as you didn't eat too many. I made a game out of pumping water with the pitcher pump, jumping every time I pumped. We had cows to milk morning and night, but that cream was delish on Post Toasties.

One other job I remember was carrying a cool drink to the field to my daddy. I was always barefooted and in the summer the sand would be so hot. I would run from the shade of one cotton stalk to another. I remember crying, my feet burned so. Guess my black satin shoes were all I had.

I do not remember the storm which blew our house away, but I do remember the clouds coming and going to the cellar many times. I remember Dad carrying me, and how dark I thought the night was.

One vivid memory I have is when Ray was so sick and Aunt Stella was there. Mama had washed some of Ray's little aprons and hung them on the orchard fence behind our house. One had blown off in the orchard, and I had a long stick trying to get the dress, which I remember so well was a tiny blue-checked [one] with a red duck embroidered on the front of it. I heard my parents cry out, I ran in and my daddy hugged me to so close, but oh what joy when Ray began to revive.

Our Christmases were very simple. We did not have a tree; we hung our long stockings and always got a small bit. I remember one year Mildred and Marie got rings, and I got a strand of beads, which was ordered from Sears, but I kept them in my mouth and they melted. We just didn't do the elaborate things that people do for Christmas now, but ours were happy.

Our visits to West Texas for two summers before we moved out here were treats for us children, taking two days to go from Dallas to Nolan County. One summer we helped Roy and Clifton swat jumbo grasshoppers that were eating up their cotton.

Then when we moved to West Texas, our first year at Wastella, we lived in a two-room house, one bedroom with three big beds in it. Different times in rent houses our family was so crowded for bedrooms, sometimes six to the room. Modern families probably think it couldn't be done, but we did it, and it didn't hurt us. Also, our bathrooms were non-existent. Those old rent houses just didn't have bathrooms just a path to an outhouse with a sagging door and highly infested with all kinds of crawling things.

Our clothes were few, too. Two new school dresses for a season and a pair of shoes which I always had trouble making mine last. One time Mildred, Marie, and I had hoed for a neighbor and had enough money we thought to buy us a new pair of shoes. We went to Sweetwater to Levy's. Mildred and I found a pair that we had enough money to buy, but Marie couldn't. So the fat, bug-eyed clerk said, "I'm going to have to give you a higher priced pair." Marie said, "You would have to *give* them to me."

When we came home from school, as hungry as a bear, we changed our clothes first and then hit the dishpan full of teacakes that Mama usually had made. Neither was there a hot lunch served at school; we carried our own, biscuit, sausage, egg, bacon or whatever we had; and there was not a snack bar to get a bar of candy or a Coke. We wouldn't have had any money, even if there had been.

Our daddy worked hard and so did the rest of the family. But when half of it *[the crop]* belonged to the landowner, a living was all we had. I don't ever remember going hungry, but many times our evening meal was hot biscuits, cream gravy, butter and syrup.

My most memorable school years were at a little two-room school called Goode, south of Roscoe. We walked two miles, and it wasn't easy in cold weather or sandstorms. But we had, I believe, more dedicated teachers, several grades for each teacher, fifteen-minute class periods. Yet we learned and got a fair education. Our homework was done at our dining table with a kerosene lamp. We younger children also went to school at a little country school called Brownlee, west of Roscoe. This was a German settlement. We liked those kids, but they had an odd quirk. But I made it just fine. Our teacher, who was not German, had a daughter my age, and we chummed together. My last years in school were at Roscoe, which I never did enjoy much. We were definitely country kids, and Roscoe had some snobs. My people rented me a room in Roscoe, which I shared with Edna Mae McClain, another country girl trying to get a high school education. (I wonder whatever happened to her.) I got real sick in the fall of my junior year with intestinal flu and was out for a while. Then our family moved to Blackwell, and I did not start back to school, which I have always regretted.

There is one memory at Roscoe that I treasure very much. It was there that I became convicted of sin and realized that I needed the Savior. I made that decision one night at a Methodist meeting under an old tabernacle, which is not there anymore. I was baptized into the Baptist Church awhile later.

At Blackwell we lived on the Copeland place and as far as I know it's the only old house still standing that was once our family home, and the last place before the children began to go to work or marry and leave home. This old house is only a quarter mile from my present home, and if any of the nieces and nephews or great nieces and nephews doubt the stories we've told about the old houses we lived in, come see me. I would love to show you what we once lived in: the bedroom that Carl, Ray, J.B., Ella Mae, Juanita and myself once occupied; the cistern where we drew our drinking water; and also the board across the corner of the back porch where we set the water bucket and dipper. It's still there. The old smokehouse still stands, so does the outhouse. It has been relocated, but it's there. The original barn is there, though it has had some work done on it, but the shed where we milked our cows is gone and also the chicken house. The old silo foundation has been made into a water tank.

After we moved to Blackwell, I met and married Bill McRorey on September 12, 1934. Our courtship was mostly in the cotton patch. The families worked together a lot. Bill and I would take rows together and would get ahead of the rest. How is that for a romantic courtship? Then he would walk to my house at night. We played forty-two some. Occasionally a traveling tent show would come to Blackwell, and we would go to that with his parents. I plunked on a guitar a little and we sang a lot. Occasionally, we got his dad's car and would drive around. But we were happy.

Our folks were all picking cotton the day we married. We quit from Wednesday for the rest of the week. We went to Roscoe and the old Baptist preacher Rev. G.W. Parks married us in his home. He had to go spit out his snuff. He said his wife was upstairs quilting, but he didn't bother to call her, so we had no witnesses, just Bill and me and the preacher. We went to Grandpa and Grandma Lewis's for dinner. Roy and Betty Mae lived in the house with them between Roscoe and Sweetwater. They had pinto beans for dinner and Grandma was making teacakes. Rolling the dough out on the table and cutting them with a biscuit cutter. They were a spice dough, and the spice was coarse ground so Grandma was picking specks out of them and said "I'm picking sticks out of these things."

Bill and I went on to Sweetwater and bought us a bill of groceries, eight dollars' worth, and you wouldn't believe what all we got, compared to today's prices. I remember we spent a penny each in a weighing machine. I weighed 128, and he weighed 142. Bill had already bought us a cute little bedroom suite, a rocking chair, and we had gathered up enough stuff elsewhere to furnish the little three-room house that was to be our home on his daddy's place. We had it all finished and ready to go to after we married. He bought the bedroom suite at Elrod's furniture store in Sweetwater, and Mr. Elrod gave us a small table which is still in our cellar with a crippled leg. Think I'll restore it and bring it out and use it. I was so pleased with our home and the only new furniture I ever owned. How I enjoyed keeping that little house. We had no water, and Bill hauled it in a barrel on a sled. That barrel was nearly always empty. In the summer we had a little rock bottom place in the creek that was our bath house. The only trouble, you had to scamper when you heard a car coming for you could be seen from the road.

In October of 1936 we suffered quite a blow in our young married life. Bill was in an accident that others have told about and lost an eye. We were faced with hospital stays, going to Dallas to St. Paul's Hospital for special surgery. I shall never forget how alone I felt that day Bill was in surgery, not knowing a soul. But Mama had written Aunt Bird, her sister, and she came and spent the day with me. Oh, never was I so glad to see someone I knew. I stayed at a little hotel across the street from the hospital, but I was so afraid. A stair case opened out into the street, and I did not feel safe even behind locked doors.

Our married lifestyle was very similar to the way we grew up, not much money. We had to work hard. We grew and canned a lot of what we ate, milked cows, raised chickens and pigs, anything to help out. But we had grown up like that and didn't mind. We were happy.

Ella Mae, Juanita, Ray, and J.B. used to come and spend a week with us in the summer. Our entertainment was what we could do at home. We played in the creek, and we all had slingshots and we would hunt and shoot wasp nests. One time I remember Ray and J.B. were here, and Bill was plowing. We found some big old perch in the creek. Couldn't find any fish hooks so Ray and J.B. made some hooks out of straight pins and we caught a mess of perch and had them fried and on the table when Bill came home.

Billie Nell, our first child, was born in December of 1937. Oh, we thought she was so pretty, and she was such a joy to us. She was born at home. We had a good old country doctor, J. W. Reynolds. I'm afraid if I faced the same situation now, I would lose my nerve. Billie Nell was the first grandchild. I think my brothers and sisters thought she was alright, too. They had moved to Busby, but Bill and I finally got an old 1928 gray-color Dodge, and we were able to go visit some, and they would come to see us, too. I remember one Easter egg hunt we had when Mama and Dad hid the eggs across the creek from our house. The rest of us all hunted eggs. Bill and I went back the next week and kept finding eggs.

In September of 1944, Larry Lewis [McRorey] was born, another at-home birth, with the same old country doctor. He was such a husky little boy, and we were so proud of him. Then in May of 1947, Charlotte was born, another precious little girl to us, not so pretty as the others. She was yellow and looked a little jaundiced. But by that time I had lost my nerve, and she was born in the Sweetwater hospital. Our three days in the hospital cost us $47; Dr. Loeb charged $75.

We went through some very hard years in the 1930s and the 1950s, especially the '50s. We were older, and it bothered us more with three children in school. I made most of their clothes, many from feed sacks, but they were colorful and pretty. But most people didn't have any better than us. Many times we wondered how we could manage, but we did. Bill's dad was good to us. Sometimes he would lease the land for oil and would help the kids some. It was in the '50s that he got a little money and put in our first bathroom. I remember so well, Billie Nell was playing ball and had gone off to a game. We took Larry and Charlotte to meet her bus. We always had to wait longer than we thought was necessary, but when Billie Nell got there, Larry and Charlotte's greeting was: "Hey Bid," as they called her, "we are going to get a bathroom." She said, "Are we?" Thanks to Bill's daddy we enjoyed it so much. Bill had to work away from home some for grocery money, and the kids and I tried to keep the weeds hoed, which at times were bigger than we were. Larry learned to drive the tractor and plowed some, too.

I went to work at the school in 1959 which eased the money pressure a little. Finally, in 1968 we were able to build the house we now live in. We did a lot of the work ourselves. Took us a year before we could move in, but we have enjoyed it so much.

I have not told about so many of our sad times, but we had them. We lost our brother Carl in the prime of life. We lost our Mother and Daddy. Bill and I have lost a little three-year-old granddaughter, and Bill has lost his parents and a sister. Yes, many tears have been mingled with our joys, but someone has said that if the eyes had no tears, the soul would have no rainbow. So through it all we have clung to the Old Rugged Cross and the One who is able to sustain us in all things. That would be my plea and desire for all who read this.

Now Bill and I have retired, all of our children are married, and we have eight grandchildren. I hope the poet knew what he was talking about when he said, "Come grow old with me, the best is yet to be."

Edna Myrtle "Myrt" Lewis McRorey
Blackwell, Texas
1979

Myrt McRorey, John Lewis and Ella Mae Whitworth at the Copeland place house where they lived fifty years earlier near Blackwell.

CHAPTER SIX

Ella Mae Lewis Whitworth

Memories of my childhood and these fifty-five years have been happy ones. This consists of good parents, love, hard work and fun. We had some tragedies as all families do.

I was born in Seagoville, Texas, August 30, 1922, but my first memories are of West Texas where we moved from East Texas when I was about three years old. As I think back my first memories are of the Forrester place, southwest of Roscoe. We rented the farms where we lived, but that really never mattered to us young ones because it was always home to us.

Mother always said she had three sets of children. Mildred, Marie, and Myrt have always been grown to me. Our family couldn't have had better sisters than we had. Never do I ever remember any of them spanking me. If they did, I am sure I needed it. One time, though, Mildred was trying to teach me how to work a written arithmetic problem. She had explained and explained, and when she was finished, she asked me if I understood, and I said "No." She may have spanked me then, and I wouldn't have blamed her now. I never did like to study. My mind was on sports most of the time, and that was what I loved most about school.

Back to our older sisters, I can just imagine them being the family for several years then here comes Dad and Mother's second set: Carl, myself and Ray, each one just a little over a year apart. What a drastic change that must have made. I have wondered many times how many little dirty bottoms, noses and faces they cleaned and, oh, how much it must have helped Mother. They were Dad's right hand "men" in the field, too. They were such hard workers and helped him put food on our table that he couldn't have done without them.

I headed maize, hoed and picked cotton, but never did plow. I imagine Dad was afraid for me to get hold of the team and plow. The brothers did plowing, though, as they grew older.

The third set of children came on the Forrester place. J.B. arrived June 15, 1926, about three years after Ray was born. I had the whooping cough—Mother said I never missed any of the diseases at school and always brought them home to the others—when J.B. was born and, if I remember, he took it when he was two weeks old. The thing that I remember most was Mother and Dad holding him upside down by his feet trying to get the mucus out because he was too small to cough it out of his throat. Mildred remembers going with Dad to the doctor's office to get him a shot. She would hold him. I think they had to go every day for a while. Then Juanita was born on December 11, 1928.

We kids always enjoyed the walk after a rain to look over the crop. Usually, Dad, Mother and the young ones who could walk would go. One time on one of these walks, I was walking in front of our dog. Ray pulled his tail, and he bit me. I will carry that scar on my foot all my life. I was born in between the three brothers, and it seemed they delighted in aggravating me. Because of this I learned to take care of myself early in life. I could outrun any of them and give them credit for being pretty good athletes.

I always kept my Christmas toys under the head of Mother and Dad's bed. Guess there was a feeling of more protection there. One Christmas I got a little iron bed with two little dolls in it. They were so cute and I was so proud of them. One day the dolls came up missing. Then we went to Grandpa Lewis's. We cousins were in the yard playing, and Cousin Jake Lewis turned a somersault and out of his pocket came my dolls. I grabbed them, and there was no way Jake was going to get them back. I would have fought the whole bunch for my dolls. Come to find out, Carl Preston had gotten them and traded them to Jake to get to shoot his BB gun.

Christmas was a big day for us. Dad and Mother usually managed to get us one toy, fruit and Christmas candy. That was the only time we got toys. One Christmas we had a big snow. We went outside and tried to find Santa's sleigh tracks. We decided it snowed more after he came to our house and had covered his tracks. Then another time Dad got some candy other than the usual Christmas kind. It was something like peanut brittle and was so good that I ate too much and made myself sick. That should have taught me a lesson, but to this day I still eat too much.

It was on this farm where our front porch was built of wood all across the front. Oh, how I loved to slip into the older girl's bedroom and wear their high heel shoes across this porch. For some reason, the sound of those high heels made me feel ten feet tall. Mildred had the prettiest black patent pair that tied on top of her foot. Those were the ones I remember wearing the most.

I was chasing J.B. on this same porch, and he ran off and broke his arm. That didn't make me feel very good. He was probably just walking good.

Juanita was the last one of the third set of children and the baby of our family. Her birth was the only one that I remember. We small ones were hustled off to Mrs. Pope's, a neighbor, and when they came after us we had a baby sister. We thought she was so cute with pretty blonde curls. She was six years younger than me and Myrt was nearly seven years older. Guess being in between the brothers must be why I grew up such a tomboy. There was no way to be a girl playing with them.

When all the family (ten of us) would go for a visit together, Ray and I would run out looking for gallon buckets to put on the back floor of the old touring Dodge car to sit on. There just wasn't enough seats for all of us. Mildred, Marie, and Myrt would sit on the back seat. Ray and I on our buckets and Carl, J.B. and Juanita would sit up front with Dad and Mother. We sure enjoyed those trips. If it was cold Mother would take quilts. We would cover up head and toe. I would peep out every once in awhile to see where we were, all just as happy as we could be.

We started picking cotton early in life as that was one thing we could do. And every pound any of us picked just helped out that much. Our first cotton sack was made out of a forty-pound flour sack. Then as we grew we used a tow sack. Then Mother would take the good part of Dad and the older girls' worn out sacks and make us one. Then came the year I got my first brand new one. Oh, how proud I was of that new sack. The first day I used it, I remember so well trying to see how much it would hold. So, I would sit down on the ground and put my feet in the sack and pack it just as much as possible. When we weighed it, there was forty pounds in there. Boy did I feel like I had really done something.

My schooling began at the two-room schoolhouse south of Roscoe, Texas, called Goode. My first teacher was Miss Ila Towe. I believe the other teacher was Miss Vera Pitts, who still lives at Roscoe. I don't remember very much about the first year, but I am sure if they played any kind of ball, I was in that. We walked to and from school most of the time, and I remember those awful sandstorms that we had to walk home in a few times. My, but how those little flying pebbles and sand would just seem to cut into our legs, but we had so much fun walking those two miles with the neighbor kids and all of us.

We moved north of Roscoe from the Forrester place to the Younger place. We all went to Roscoe School. I didn't like that school. It seems most of my class were city kids, and there was sure a difference back then in country kids and city kids. We were happy, but just as poor as anyone, and Mother or Mildred made our undies out of those forty-pound flour sacks. Those sacks were used for a lot of things. The "Gold Chain" brand didn't always wash out so it may have shown somewhere on those undies. Anyway, those girls in my class would play baseball at recess time and would line up to bat. I would try to get in line, and they would push me out. I am sure I would cry, and they would make fun of me.

There was this one little girl that had what we called finger curls that hung long and bounced up and down like a spring when she walked. She was the ring leader of the bunch. I went home one evening crying and told Dad how she pushed me out of line and wouldn't let me play. He told me to grab hold of one of those curls and give it a big yank. I was afraid it would get me into trouble so wouldn't dare. We were taught to be nice and not get into trouble, and that was the only time I remember Dad every telling me to do anything ugly. With my training from my brothers, I probably could have whipped her though. As I grew, sin would creep into my mind, and I wished I had of *[whipped her]*. Since then, it always did hurt me to see some kid running over another one. I worked in the Young People's Department in our church and used that experience, maybe too much, in devotions, but that has always stayed with me and taught me about God as a respecter of persons. He loved all, rich, poor, and color. We should do the same.

One day all of us girls and Mother went to see a neighbor. I don't remember her name. While Mother and the older girls visited, I played outside. As everyone's bathroom was outside, one with a path *[from the house]*. Making a trip there, I discovered a brand new catalogue. Must have just been put there as very few pages were torn out and, oh, it had some of the best-looking paper dolls. I wanted that catalogue so bad that I made several trips to the house to ask the lady for it, but my heart would always fail me. I was so afraid Mother would get on me. Finally, time came to go home, and I knew it was then or never, so finally I raked up the courage to ask her. She was so gracious to give it to me, and Mother didn't spank me. Mother let me sit up later than usual that night and burn some of the kerosene oil that we had to be so saving with in our lamp to cut out paper dolls. I had boy dolls, girl dolls and baby dolls. I would spend hours playing with them until Ray found them, and he just delighted in tearing their heads off. He and John were talking just recently, and Ray said he remembered how he loved tearing them off, I am sure to aggravate me mostly. Anyway, I sure had some good times until he found them.

We lived by some neighbors, the Bryants. Mr. Bryant was a small man, if I remember right. One day he was outside where we kids were playing, and he said he would give me a nickel if I would outrun any of the boys. That was right down my alley, and I won that nickel, which was as much as a dollar or more these days, and I was proud of it. It could have been my first nickel.

We moved on to the Woodard place, west of Roscoe in the Brownlee community. This neighborhood was mostly German people. They were good, hard-working, saving people. When we started to Brownlee school, our principal's family, the Harrisons, and our family were the only Americans. Those German kids had the best time around us talking in their language where we couldn't understand what they were saying. We really enjoyed that school. They were all good to us, and that's where my ball playing really began. The girls wore striped overalls a lot, and when I finally got a pair, I was so proud of them. I always did like to wear the boy's overalls, but I wasn't allowed to do that much, and they didn't have that many so when I got a pair of my very own, I really thought I had something.

We played baseball during recesses, and I loved every minute of it. Most of my time was spent doing just that, and that took care of most of my education. I never did like to study and still don't very much. If I just passed my grades, that satisfied me. One day when we got our report cards to my surprise there was a big "B" in deportment. (I don't know what it's called now.) Anyway, I knew a spanking was next. Oh, how I dreaded going home. Dad and Mother weren't there when we got home, but they came in a short time later. It seemed like hours to me, though, and when I saw them coming, I ran to the barn thinking to hide, but I realized the sooner I got it over with the better. So I went back to the house to take my punishment. To my surprise Dad didn't spank me, but he said if I didn't make an "A" the next time then a spanking would come. I knew that's exactly what he meant, so I had another long wait. I sure was a good girl during that time, too. I did exactly what the teacher said. Boy, I was never any prouder of an "A" than that one. I remember so well why I got that "B." I was getting up from my desk to write on the blackboard without the teacher's permission. One of those times, she hit me on the head with her pencil. So, there was no doubt why the "B" was on my report card. I just didn't think too much about it until it was too late.

I had learned to whistle between my teeth from my brothers, and walking home from school one day I came out with a loud whistle. The kids thought that was something for a girl and asked me to do it again, and I was real happy to oblige them. I sure felt big and nearly every evening someone asked me to whistle.

It was on this place we had company come in, and Mother asked me to run to the garden. I ran out the back door and instead of going down the steps, I jumped them and landed on a mesquite thorn. Marie came and pulled it out as I couldn't. I went on to the garden. After dinner it really began to hurt. If I put my weight on it, it sure did hurt. I didn't think I could walk to the field that evening. After our company left everyone went except me. Dad thought maybe I was using my foot as an excuse, but it really did hurt. Our medicine was bought mostly from Watkins or Rawleigh salesmen that came to people's home selling. Well, we had that ol' Rawleigh's red salve that Dad thought was a cure-all. It was a pretty deep plum color red but, oh, how it did burn and us kids hated that ol' red stuff. Anyway, out it came and on my foot it went. I cried all night long, not from hurt, but from burning. I was sleeping with Myrt upstairs. What a miserable night she must have had. Mother made me come down and wash my foot, but that didn't help much. The next morning there was a blister between my toes. Dad had threatened to spank me if I didn't hush and go to sleep, and he felt bad about it when he saw the blister. For three weeks I suffered and finally Dad took me to Dr. Young in Roscoe and he lanced it. The toe next to my little one swelled so bad that the skin on it split. It is stiff to this day. When I think back, though, I am thankful I didn't lose my foot. I remember Mother fixed the old rocking chair with some quilts and pillows for me to sleep by her bed. I had to keep my foot elevated so it wouldn't throb so.

Myrt, I guess being the youngest of the older girls, slept with Juanita and myself. Mildred and Marie usually slept in what we called the front bedroom. The three boys slept together. Myrt always took water that she sat on the floor by our bed as one of us had to have a drink during the night.

We had an old mule when we lived on this farm that didn't want to leave the barn. When you got on him, he would start backing up. We were some distance from the mailbox and would ride this mule sometimes. The boys learned if they would head him down the road backwards, he would back so far then they could turn him around, and he would go to the mailbox.

Dad had set the old car up for winter. He put it under a shed in the barn. Somehow, a large hole (one of us could have fallen through while playing in the barn) was in the top just above the driver's seat. The top was made of some type of canvas. Come spring Dad got the car running and came driving it to the house. As he stopped, he stuck his head out the hole. We all got so tickled. I remember how Mother laughed.

We made a good crop on this place in 1932. If I remember, we made seventy-six bales of cotton. We would start first picking the cotton when it began to open. It would be too green to pull, but as it became drier we could pull it, and how glad we were because it was so much easier. We would have to pull over the same field two or three times and sometimes four. When we would move from one field to another, how we would wish we were through instead of moving to another field.

It was after that crop we moved to Blackwell. That was a long way from Roscoe to Blackwell—about thirty-six miles—to us, and we thought we'd never get there. We sure had some good times on this place which adjoined the McRorey farm. They were good neighbors, and so their boys began courting our sisters. Our move to Blackwell turned out okay for our family. We enjoyed the creek that ran through our place. Most of us learned to swim and also dive off the banks of this creek. We spent most of our time when we didn't have to work swimming. We sure had lots of fun.

Carl had learned to drive by this time. I guess the top to the car had torn up and there was none on it. Carl liked to drive to the mailbox and Juanita loved to go with him. One time as they were coming back, Carl always drove around back of the house so that he made a "U" turn around the woodpile, and Juanita fell out. I can't remember it hurting her, though. I imagine us kids laughed about it as we usually saw something funny in almost everything.

J.B. told about the Christmas when Mildred and Marie bought everything. It was the first tree I remember, and it looked so pretty. I remember so well getting my first doll with hair. She was the prettiest one I had ever seen. I also got some real garters. I had always had to cut me some out of old inner tubes. These were pink with a little rose design on them. My, how proud I was of those. I will always remember that Christmas as one of the best.

This was the place where we finally got rid of the ol' red salve. Somehow in the move from Roscoe the jar got broken. One day Myrt and I slipped it outside and buried it. I don't guess Dad or Mother ever knew what happened to it, and we sure didn't ever tell. We kids were so glad that stuff was gone.

We liked Blackwell school. It was a nice building and, with the exception of Roscoe, it was the largest one we had ever attended. There was a boy there named George Sweet, who had been to the Interscholastic League meet and won first place in running. He was kind of bragging about how good he was, so showoff me challenged him for a race and I won. Poor boy wouldn't even come back to where the other kids were watching and laughing. I sure felt like I had really done something and, as I've said, sports were my favorite.

One time the boys had gotten some firecrackers. It may have been the Christmas Mildred and Marie had. Anyway, one of them had the idea of putting one under a gallon bucket, letting only the fuse stick out from under it, sitting on the bucket and lighting the fuse. Sure enough when it went off, it was quite an explosion and needless to say they didn't try that again as it left the ring print of the bucket on his seat.

There was never a dull moment with my brothers. We caught an armadillo one time and decided to keep him for a pet. So we put him under a tub and, of course, he dug out and was gone the next morning. We didn't know they could dig so well, so one night ended that.

Dad and his brothers loved to go fishing. One time they did what they called grappling for fish. They would find some large rocks *[where catfish hid]* and would grab them and bring them up. This time I'm thinking about, Dad lost his billfold, and all the money we had was in there. He had to borrow enough money to get us by until the first bale of cotton. I just can't imagine now not having one penny and a family of ten, but that was the way we lived back then.

I remember Mother's sister, Aunt Ethel, and her family coming to see us. They were the only ones of Mother's people I knew for a long time and the only ones who came to see us much. Years later, her sister, Aunt Bird, came. I've never seen any of Mother's brothers. Aunt Bird and Uncle Fred are the only two living now, I believe. I never knew her Daddy or Mother. So memories of her family are few. Most of Dad's people lived out here, though, so we saw them pretty often.

We moved to the Busby community from Blackwell. This move didn't seem so long because we had an idea how far it was this time. I'll never forget the first day we went to Busby school. We were about two and a half miles from school when we got to a neighbor's house (the Barkley's), and their kids came out and walked with us. It sure made our first day better. They were real nice to us and had a girl about my age named Marie that I became good friends with. It wasn't long until we knew everyone.

This was the first school where I played basketball. I was a guard and went on to Roby school later and really got into basketball. I won several little basketballs, one pin and a trophy. They gave these at tournaments where we played at different schools. I sure enjoyed all those games. We also played tennis and baseball, my favorite, at Busby. My position in baseball was pitcher. I don't mean to brag on myself, but I was thought to be a good pitcher. Still I give credit to our brothers because I had to be pretty tough to defend myself. Anyway, we were playing the community of Moody. Later after I was grown, I was talking to Mrs. Pittman, a teacher at Moody at that time, and she told me they used to wish I'd had chicken pox or something so I couldn't pitch, and they could beat us. I was not very popular with the boys as far as being their girlfriend, so I was glad my sports gave me some popularity.

We kids were just like most kids. When Dad and Mother would go into town for groceries we would sometimes get into mischief. This time I'm thinking about we were going to make some fudge candy. As I've said before, we would buy some products from the Watkins and Rawleigh companies *[representatives]* that came to the homes selling. The Watkins vanilla and liniment were in bottles just alike, and Ray got the liniment instead of the vanilla. When we put it into the hot fudge, we knew immediately it was the wrong bottle. We decided to take the fudge out in the field by the east side of our house and bury it. We were afraid to try another batch because Dad and Mother might get back before we could finish. We had things washed and back in place when they came home. Every time Dad would plow out where we buried the candy, we would get tickled and wonder if he might stick a plow.

We had an ol' mean rooster. Every time we were outside and he caught our backs to him, he would run and jump on the back of our legs with his spurs. Most of the time, he would draw blood. One time I was outside and saw him watching me, so I picked up a stick and turned my back, playing like I wasn't watching, when all the time I had my eyes on him. Sure enough here he came. Just as he made his attack, I hit him as hard as I could with that stick. I sure thought I'd killed him because he fell over, out like a light. It wasn't long, though, that he began to come to and began going around in a small circle and every circle he made got larger until he finally made it to the chicken house. I never was bothered again by that rooster.

One time Mother made a cake with some creamy white icing. She let us kids scrape the pan. We were all busy trying to get a bite, and Carl spied the lard bucket. He dipped out a spoon of lard and asked Ray if he wanted that bite. Ray did, and did we all have a laugh, except Ray, but Ray got me back for laughing. We were all in the field working. I had some bubble gum that I had chewed and stuck under the table at noon. I forgot to get it when we went back to work. Running out of drinking water, Dad sent Ray to the house to refill our jug. I asked him to bring my gum. He made a hole in it and put black pepper in it then smoothed it over again so I wouldn't notice. It didn't take long chewing it until WOW! I could have whipped him for ruining my gum and should have. For a long time after that when I chewed bubblegum, it seemed I could still taste black pepper.

One day we were playing at the barn. We had a mare that was standing up asleep. Ray walked up behind her and gave her a pat.

She kicked him in the stomach. She was a gentle mare, but because she was asleep, I guess, was why she kicked. Ray vomited most of the night. He sure was sick and Mother sat up with him.

We always milked several cows. Mother made butter for us and sold all she could to help on grocery bills. She kept the milk in gallon buckets and had put several on one end of the table. The table was one of those with the large center leg. She was going to skim the cream, which would rise to the top. The table toppled over and milk went everywhere. We kids thought it was funny and couldn't understand why Mother cried, but I am sure she lost several pounds of butter. We went to the cottonseed bin and got a large scoop to shovel up the spilt milk.

There was a large hole as big as a room in one of our fields. I don't remember why it was there, but we would go out here and drag up lots of tumbleweeds and throw them in the hole. Dad would set it afire at night. It would really light up around and we kids really enjoyed this.

When I was about fourteen, Dad and Mother bought me a pair of brown and white dress shoes that had a higher heel than I had ever had for my very own. I was out on the front porch with them on and, of all things, fell off the porch and broke the heel off one. My heart was just broken. I was probably doing some proud walking and not watching what I was doing. I don't remember if it hurt me, but I sure remember the heel of that shoe.

There was sadness on this place for our family. It was in the fall of 1936. Dad was putting up a wind-charger on top of the house so we could have electricity. We were so excited that we would have some lights and radio. Bill and Myrt were there, and Uncle Clyde (Dad's brother) and Aunt Ione came to help. Also Dub Elam, a friend of Carl's was there. They had it wired and wanted the wind-charger turned on to see if it was working. They didn't have the wires hooked up so electricity was just making sparks. The wind was high so as soon as the sparks began, they yelled to turn it off. Bill, Carl, and Dub all ran to cut it off. The cut-off wire broke in the process. Bill thought he would crawl up on the house and stop it before it could get going too fast. He crawled up the edge and just got a little too close. When he looked up, the propeller hit him in the face. This happened so fast, and I had run outside to see which one of the boys got to cut it off. I watched as Bill got closer to the wind charger, but just couldn't yell at him. The way I remember, I just froze. When it hit Bill, I did scream and all came running. Myrt ran up the ladder just like it was stairs. It had been raining for several days and the roads were so muddy. Uncle Clyde's Model A Ford was the only car that would start, so he, Dad, Bill, and Myrt started to Sweetwater. I believe they said it took two and a half hours to drive the ten miles. I don't know what time this happened, but it was nearly dark when they got back home. Dad told us Bill was going to be okay but he had lost his eye. I have often wondered if I'd hollered at Bill if he would have stopped and maybe this wouldn't have happened. Carl was standing behind the wood heater when Dad told us, and he turned around his face to the wall and cried his heart out. He was fifteen then and little did we realize that about a year later we would lose him.

Carl was going to Roby school and playing football. He was sixteen years old, weighed 180 pounds and was a good player. They were playing the last game of the season, I think, at Colorado City. One of the Roby players tackled an opponent and was slung around, his leg hit the back of one of Carl's legs on the calf below his knee. A large Roby man they called Tiny Hammonds brought him home. Carl told Dad he thought his leg was broken, but he was tired and wanted to wait until the next morning to go to the doctor. The next morning I remember putting his socks on him to get him ready to go. The doctor found the small bone broken and said it was overlapped about an inch. Carl said he made another play after he was hurt. The doctor told Dad Carl would limp if he didn't operate and put the bone back in place. The ether they gave him to put him to sleep made him sick. He vomited and sucked some ether into his lungs and developed pneumonia. He was so sick and died on Thanksgiving Day in 1937. The doctor said his heart had been in such a strain from football all season and was not strong enough to take it. He said if they had only known and waited a week he thought he would have made it. Dad and Mother always wondered, but I guess it was God's plan even though we couldn't understand why. I was fifteen then, just one year and twenty-six days younger than Carl. We missed him so much, and Mother grieved so. We lost her nearly five years later.

I met and married Joe Whitworth while we lived on this place. He and his brother Jack farmed their place to the east of us. The first time I met Joe, he came by and wanted us to help them finish picking the last of their cotton. He was going on to town and was to come by and pick up Ray, J.B. and me. Dad told us we could help them. Joe had a Model A coupe with a rumble seat. I told Ray and J.B. that I was not going to ride up front with Joe, that one of them could, and I'd ride in the rumble seat with the other. I thought that was settled, but when Joe came back, Ray said, "Eller, you ride up front with Joe, and J.B. and I will ride in the rumble seat." Oh, how I could have shook them, but rather than embarrass us all, I rode up front. Little did I know Joe would later be my husband. We began dating the summer of 1939. I was going to Roby school and was in my sophomore year. When I was a junior, I wanted to quit school. It was during basketball season. My coach, Miss Selman, who also taught my English and speech classes, asked me if I would please finish the basketball season. She was such a nice person and good coach so I finished that year. Of course, I had marrying on my mind, and I didn't think I needed any more education. I found out later schooling sure wouldn't have hurt any.

Joe and I dated for over a year. Our first date was to my first rodeo. It was at the Double Heart Ranch south of Sweetwater. Joe came after me in his Model A Ford. He didn't talk much, and I didn't either, but either there was no glasses in the doors or he had them both rolled down, and I didn't know to roll mine up. Anyway, my hair was blowing topsy-turvy, and I said I wish I had something to tie my hair down. He said he had a lariat in the rumble seat. He took me to my first cafe to eat. That was quite a treat for me.

One time they were having a box supper at the community of Capitola where Ralph Ammons taught school. Ralph was to help with the selling of the boxes. Marie made a pretty box of purple and yellow crepe paper. The women made some real pretty boxes. They would put food in them. Marie didn't want just anyone buying her box because the women ate with who bought their box. So, she asked Joe if he would buy her box, and he told her he would. So she put enough food for the three of us. Well, there were several boxes sold before Marie's. Joe didn't bid on any until Marie's came up. He began at once and two men there thought it was my box so they began bidding to make Joe really pay for "my" box. When they finally let him have it the bid was seven dollars and fifty cents. That was a lot of money back then, but Joe said he had twenty dollars and intended to buy that box if that would do it. Marie spread the food, we ate, and Joe and I left. As we walked out of the lighted schoolhouse and into dark, we couldn't see anything and ran head-on into a car. Joe and I got so tickled, and he teased Marie later about what she put in her box.

Joe took me to several rodeos. I always did like western clothes, and when I was growing up my ideal husband was to be a cowboy, live on a big ranch. It didn't turn out quite like that. One time the Whitworths were camping and fishing on the Santa Fe Lake just north of Sweetwater. Joe came after me, and we went by where they were. Olene, Jack Whitworth's wife, had made what Joe called a chocolate pudding. It was like a chocolate pie only she put it in a large pan and didn't have a crust. Joe ate about half of it. She always could make good chocolate puddings. We had some real good times on this lake fishing after we married. We have caught some nice fish, too. The Whitworth families all loved to fish. One time we had laid a tablecloth on the ground and spread our food on that, then we all sat on the ground around the spread. Jack said, "Ella Mae, I want to sit by you because I know the food will be coming your way." I always have liked to eat.

Joe and I married December 24, 1940. We lived with the Whitworths for about three weeks, then moved to Coleman, Texas. Joe was working for the Santa Fe railroad as a section hand. His job in Sweetwater played out and there was an opening in Coleman. We carried everything we owned in that rumble seat of Joe's Model A. He had his granddaddy Whitworth's trunk that we put our things in. There was one small room that was empty in the section house. We went to a secondhand store and bought a three-burner, kerosene cook stove and a small oven that would set on and off the stove; also a small table and two chairs; iron bed with springs; and mattress. We had some dishes, pots and pans, water bucket and dipper that we had gotten in our shower. So that was our first home. We got some wooden apple boxes for a cabinet and washstand. A big railroad nail driven into the wall was our clothes closet. The trunk was our chest of drawers. We were just as happy as if we had a mansion.

We came back to Sweetwater pretty often as we didn't know anyone in Coleman, only those living in the section house. One night we were lonesome and decided to go to the show. It had been raining and the street in front of the section house would get so muddy. Joe thought we could make it, but we got stuck. Joe got out to push, and I was to drive. He put the car in neutral and left the motor running. I didn't know very much about driving so I just moved over, took the steering wheel and began giving it the gas. I thought I was doing all the good only we weren't moving. Joe came up to the window and said, "Ella Mae, did you put it in gear?" Well, I hadn't and when I did with Joe pushing we moved right on out. Joe didn't say anything, but I know he could have shook me good.

One of my most embarrassing moments was when we lived in Coleman. We went to see this couple we had met and didn't know very well. Joe wore his overalls that he wore most of the time. Our conversation had run out, and I was trying to keep it going so I asked them if they had seen Joe with his overalls off. What I should have said was "Have you seen Joe other than in his overalls?" The couple didn't know what to say, and when I tried to correct what I said I just made it worse. So, needless to say, we went home shortly thereafter.

The first night we spent in Coleman the section house was next to the railroad, and there was a passenger train that came through about 10 p.m. We were sound asleep, and when that train came through with its whistle wide open we almost left out. When we really realized what it was, we were both sitting up in bed hanging on to each other for dear life. I will never forget that. It took us several weeks before we got used to the trains.

Mother really took sick while we lived in Coleman. I took my turn with the other girls staying a week at a time to take care of her. She wasn't able to get out of bed for about a year. She was so sorry that us girls had to stay away from our homes to help take care of her, but back then that's the way people took care of the sick. We were glad to do it for our mother, even though we did miss our homes. Our mother was such an understanding person. We missed her so much. There were so many times I'd loved to have talked to her. She was the kind of person we could have talked to in strict confidence.

Mother died September 9, 1942, and in October of that year Joe and I moved back from Coleman and into the house with Dad, J.B. and Juanita. Joe helped farm the place. We lived there through the next fall, then Joe went back to work for the railroad. We moved in an upstairs apartment at Mrs. Freeman's. It was on the same road going to Dad's, only about two miles north of Sweetwater.

We bought four lots, in what was called the Eastridge addition in Sweetwater and built a four-room and bath home. We moved in May of 1946 and have lived here since that time. In May of 1966 we remodeled and added another room, bath and carport. I am proud of our home and after living here this long, it would be hard to think of living somewhere else.

Joe's railroad job played out again, and he worked at the U.S. Gypsum Mill for a short time loading sheetrock. He then went to work for Mr. C.C. Justiss Sr. drilling water wells. He worked for him about eight years. Joe has said he learned what he knew about drilling wells from Mr. Justiss. He then worked for Jack Stewart drilling wells, and he bought his own drilling rig in 1956. Joe really enjoyed this work. He did most of it by himself. His nephew Carl Lewis (Ray's oldest son) helped him two summers when he was about fourteen and fifteen. Then another nephew Marc Lewis (J.B.'s youngest son) helped him some in the summer. He had another boy, Jim Bob Watts, that helped him two summers, but other than that I was his helper. I never did make a very good hand, but I would do when he couldn't get anyone else. We would move from one location to another. After we got the rig set up, Joe didn't need me until he was ready to move again.

I did help him set up the windmill towers. I never did like that job, and I was always so glad when we got it set up and cemented down. I helped him work on windmills, too. This was where we had most of our problems. One time we were cleaning out a well, and Joe had me off in a bedded field with a cable tied on the front of the pickup letting the bailer in and out of the well. Once, I got the pickup off the beds that I was supposed to stay on and was trying to get back on them and was not watching and hit the top of the tower with the bailer. Joe took off out from under that tower, and when he tucked his head and started my way I knew I was in for a good one. But by the time he got to where the pickup was, I had time to have my speech ready. So, I told him I knew what I did was dangerous and wouldn't do it again. One time like that when you realize someone could have been hurt is lesson enough. Joe just said *do* be careful and went back to the mill. I was glad when that job was done. We worked at some real pretty places. I would see deer, turkey and other animals and lots of birds. Then some places were really rough to get to. That rig was a good one and made us a good living. Joe sold it in August 1977. He still misses it, but it was just getting to be too much work for him.

Most of our pleasure have been hunting and fishing. I have had some of the best times. We have fished a lot at Junction on the Llano River; also have gone to the Rio Grande River and several lakes. Joe has hunted in Colorado. He and Ralph went one year, and he killed a large elk. He was so proud of that hunt. He had the hide tanned and Mildred made him a coat. Preston Lewis asked for that coat or jacket, and Joe told him he could have it after he was through with it. Joe and I both love to hunt deer and have killed several. We dress them ourselves and put them in the deep freezer. We have venison all year. It sure is good. We have hunted, too, in New Mexico for the last three years. Ray, Maxine, J.B., Jurdene and us take our trailers. We sure have had some good times up there in those mountains. One can sure see God's creations out in the mountains and on the rivers. His beauty is all around you, and I have enjoyed every minute of it.

The first church service I remember attending was in the Brownlee schoolhouse. The only thing that stands out in my mind was the song that was sung, "Oh, Happy Day." We don't hear it much anymore, but I will always like that song as a special one. I don't remember going when we lived at Blackwell, but after we moved to Busby, Carl, the brother we lost, would take us. Then after we lost him, Daddy and Mother went with us. This was Liberty Baptist Church. It was here that I met the Lord and was saved. My, how good that makes you feel and such a different outlook on life. I still had problems, but they were so much easier to solve. Liberty Church will always be a precious memory to me. When we moved to Sweetwater, I started going to Lamar Street Baptist Church, and in 1948 Joe was saved there. We still attend that church.

Our family was blessed with some singing talent. Most of us have sung in the choir in our churches and enjoy singing together. Several of our nieces and nephews sing, too, and some play the guitar. I am so proud of all of them.

I am so thankful that Dad and Mother instilled in us right from wrong and loved us so much that my remembrances of childhood are happy ones. I am so proud of my family, the nieces, nephews, and their children. How I look forward to our reunion and seeing everyone each summer. I thank the Lord for the good life I've had and often have wondered why I was blessed so graciously. It has been such a pleasure to write of my childhood and growing up. There have been so many things that came to my mind that I haven't thought of in so many years and so many that I couldn't write them all, but I have tried to the best of my knowledge to write the things that stand out in my mind the most. I have enjoyed every minute of it as it was kind of re-living my life over again. I have finished this April 20, 1978, and wish all a very full, happy life.

Love always,
Ella Mae Lewis Whitworth
Sweetwater, Texas
1978

CHAPTER SEVEN

Ray Franklin Lewis

The blessed event that happened on November 13, 1923, at the N.P. Lewis household I don't remember a lot about. In fact, I'm not sure I remember a whole lot prior to starting to school in the first grade in Roscoe. It seems to me that I can remember a picture that someone has of Carl Preston and Ella Mae sitting in a mud puddle and me on a tricycle, and I think I can remember that, but I'm not real sure. The first thing that comes to mind is the first grade at Roscoe school. It was a short day, and we had finished, I think, the activities, and a bunch of us towheaded boys were playing in the back of the schoolroom. I know in the back corner of the room a hole had been cut in the ceiling to get in the attic. Some boy grabbed my little cap I had on and threw it up in the attic, and I thought I was ruined for life. I know I started bawling, and the teacher came by and asked what was the matter? I told her and she got the janitor and retrieved the cap, and that was my first day and first experience in first grade at school.

My memories of childhood, I know, seem to always be happy ones. We certainly didn't have a lot, but there was a lot of love, and the boys and the girls seemed to get along good. I remember heading maize in sleds that Dad would make and put boxes on them. It seems to me that Mildred, Myrt and Marie were the ones that had to put up with Carl Preston, J.B., and me. We used to delight in going to the fields with a mule hooked to the sled and two of us riding in the box. If I remember right, the younger one J.B. worked with Mildred, me with Marie, and Carl with Myrt, but we boys thought it was the funniest thing in the world to get in the back of the box and wiggle the sled or turn the box over, anything to aggravate the older girls. I don't know how they put up with us as long as they did.

I remember, I think it was in '32, when we headed so much maize. It rained a lot late in the year. I know Uncle Cliff would come out to visit, and I remember going duck hunting with him where dad had cut his high gear and shocked it. I'd go out with Uncle Cliff, and he'd sit on top of one of those shocks or behind it. The old lakebeds had water in them, and he'd shoot ducks. I'd retrieve his ducks. I don't know whether I was much of a birddog, but I sure enjoyed going and getting those ducks when he knocked them down.

At the Brownlee school, the thing that sticks in my mind was there was not many families that weren't German or of German descent. I know Mr. Harrison was the school teacher, and I vividly remember one morning going to school, and he had turned out some of the high school classes. The older boys were helping him kill hogs. At the first recess, some of us small boys went out. I know Mr. Harrison had shot an old hog—he had a .22 he was shooting them with —and he'd hit him low in the snout. The old hog was running around the pen just a squealing, and we thought that was the funniest thing in the world. He finally got an axe and got on the fence. When the old hog came by, he hit him on the head and killed him. I never will forget the hog-killing episode.

I like to never got where I could pronounce a lot of the people's names. Seems to me like that most of them were Zenckes or Zetzmans or Hackfeltz or Rennafeltz. There just wasn't many kids at Brownlee I remember that were not of German descent.

I remember some place we lived, there was an old gentleman who lived down the road from us named Len Moseley, and I thought that was the fastest talking fellow I'd ever heard in my life. I know J.B. and I used to go with Dad in a wagon down to his place. We'd go to a pump station and get crude oil. What we used the crude oil for, Mother would have J.B. and me out in the chicken house. We'd have to clean manure out from under the roost and then paint the roost with that crude oil. I think it was to kill the lice or bugs of some kind. That used to be a bad job, me and him thought, of having to paint that roost with stinking crude oil.

I also remember what fun we had walking to school at Brownlee up the railroad track. I know one time there was a train that derailed at a little bridge, and there was a boxcar or two that had apples and oranges. I know we picked up a few apples and oranges, and we thought that was some treat. But we'd walk those rails to school to see who could walk the rail the farthest. Best I remember, none of us could walk it very far, but as we got more practice we were able to go several hundred yards down the track just walking the rails.

I remember very well when we moved from Roscoe to Blackwell, I rode on a wagon and team with Uncle Cliff. He had a wagon loaded with implements of some kind—planters and cultivators, I guess—but just prior to our move there a tornado had come through by Highland. Of course, on the move we went from Roscoe to Highland and on to Blackwell through Maryneal. There were still signs of the trees being blown down and there was straw sticking in some of the trees. I'd always heard of the force the wind of a tornado had blowing stuff into trees, but Uncle Cliff explained to me that really wasn't the way it was. He said the wind would be so high the trees would twist; and cracks would come in the bark; and the straw would get wedged in there; and when the wind died down they'd straighten up. It looked like the straw was blown into the trunk. I always remember him explaining that to me, and I always appreciated him telling me just how that happened because being a kid I thought that was the wind being high enough to wedge that straw into a tree. I know I thought that was the longest trip. I thought we were moving plumb out of the country. Of course, it was probably about thirty miles by Highland, through Maryneal and on to Blackwell, but you got into the trees and some timber. I thought that we were in hog heaven when we got to Blackwell and moved into that old house with that little creek down there where it had running water most of the time.

I'll never forget a Christmas we had there when Mildred and Marie were working. I thought it was the best Christmas we ever had. J.B. and I got a little red wagon together. We also got some trucks that had headlights on them. I remember going in one of the bedrooms; of course, I don't think there was but two. But we'd go in and get under the bed and turn on the little battery-powered lights on our trucks and just run as long as they'd let us stay up running those trucks under the bed. I guess it was Christmas day we got our wagon out. The barn west of the house sat pretty close to the edge of the creek. There was a pretty good bluff there where the cows would go down to water and pasture along a cow trail that was pretty steep. We got our red wagon on top *[of the bluff]*, and we'd get on that cow trail and both of us would jump in the wagon and down the hill we'd go. Well, it wasn't long until we got to arguing about whose turn it was to guide. One of us sat in the front and the other would push us off, then he'd jump on the back end. I thought for sure it was my time to guide, and J.B. didn't think so, so he was in the front and I pushed him off and reached around and got a hold of the handle. I was gonna guide anyway a holding around him. We got messed up there, ran off the trail and hit a tree head-on with that wagon and knocked the front wheels out from under it. I never will forget how sad I thought it was we had torn our wagon up the first day we rode it, but I think we finally got us some big washers and some of dad's wrenches and put washers where it tore the hole out in the bed and got the front wheels back under it and still used it for a long time. I think that was the same wagon Juanita had tied to the cow's tail and as she came through the gate got hung up and pulled her tail off, the cow's, of course. But we did have some fine times on the creek there at Blackwell.

We all had chores to do. I know for Ella Mae and myself it was our chore to do the milking, and J.B. was supposed to go get the milk cows. Well, of course, he didn't like to go get the milk cows by himself, and he'd always want us to go with him, and that really wasn't our job. I remember one time when me and John got into it pretty good, Ella Mae and I was wanting to get through milking a little early for some reason, and John wouldn't go get the cows so we decided we'd get them, and he was gonna follow us. Man, that made us mad as the devil. Me and him got in a scrap. I know John had a scab on his nose, and I knocked the scab off his nose. If I remember right, I got a paddling when I got home. John and I were always having a scrap or two as boys, but Ella Mae and I sure felt like he ought to have gone ahead and gotten those cows so we could've milked a little earlier.

With school at Blackwell, I remember the third grade real well. Mrs. Alexander was my teacher. And at recess we'd go out to play ball. There was two of the meanest kids I believe I ever saw in my life who went to school with me in the third grade in Blackwell. One of them was Fain Whiteside and the other was Russell Walls. And those boys would rather fight as eat, and they always liked to pick on me. I guess I was a little easy, easy to whip or something. Nellie Frances Rainey was always my buddy. If it hadn't been for her, I'd never got to bat when we was playing ball at school because Fain and Russell would want to do all the batting and have us play in the outfield. But she'd get a bat and keep them away while I batted. I don't know how I would have made it through the third grade without Nellie Frances Rainey.

I also remember at Blackwell when we lived on the creek there that Dad had an old Dodge car. I don't know what model it was, probably '28 or '29, but Carl Preston had learned to drive the old Dodge. Our mailbox was up through the pasture to the north close to where Snooter Johnson lived. J.B. and myself, we'd get in that old car with Carl, and he'd drive that old Dodge up to the mailbox. We wasn't too old—I was probably ten or eleven, something like that—so he got to letting me drive, and I got to where I thought I could drive that Dodge pretty good. All I was doing was just heading it down the lane coming from the mailbox, but he's the one that taught me how to drive.

Another thing I remember at Blackwell would be playing on the creek. Man, if we weren't in school or didn't have chores to do, we'd be on the creek playing. I remember one time it was Bill McRorey and John English, I think. Of course, they were about grown, but they'd play with us on the creek. Down below the house there was a pretty good hole of water with a good sandbar by it, and we'd all just strip off buck naked and go swimming. John English and Bill McRorey would get on their hands and knees, and me and J.B. would try to ride them as horses. And, they would buck and try to throw us off in the water. If you can imagine what it would be like with a wet hiney coming out of water in that sand and getting on somebody's back; it was just like sandpaper. I guess that's the reason they bucked so high. I don't know, but they could sure throw us off pretty easy.

Another thing I remember about the creek was J.B., Ella Mae and I were always wanting to picnic on the creek when we wanted something to eat. We decided one time it was real hot. We got us some cornbread and maybe some onion, I don't remember for sure, but we went down on the creek and found a bird's nest. We decided it was hot enough to fry bird eggs on rocks so we robbed them bird's nest and tried to fry those eggs on a flat rock. The best I remember they weren't too tasty.

There was a Richards kid in Blackwell that was always my buddy, and I'd go home with him sometimes to spend the night, and he'd come home with me at other times to spend the night. What I remember about this boy was we'd have a big time playing until bedtime and as soon as we got in bed, he'd get homesick and want to go home. He'd take the earache. Dad would have to get out of bed and carry him home. He did this time after time. I don't know whether the boy ever had the earache or he was just homesick. I can sure remember taking him home several times after bedtime because of him having the earache.

We only stayed at Blackwell two or three years. I remember the move to Busby. Dad had rented from Mr. Tom Bolin a place about ten miles north of Sweetwater. And on the move to Busby, Dad either bought a red Model A Ford truck or had borrowed one, I don't remember which. But I remember Arnold carrying the cows in the truck, and I rode with him from Blackwell to Busby. As you got ready to turn into the house at Busby, it was a pretty steep hill. I know he had to get a lower gear and when he did the cows kind of went to the back end of the truck, and when they did the front end of the truck lifted off the road, the front wheels did. Like to scared me to death, but I remember him laughing about it. But we got them on up there and got them unloaded.

We had some good times at Busby. I remember soon after we got there, we were walking to school, which was about two, two-and-a-half miles *[away]*, and we'd cut across the field to go to school. This particular morning the fog was pretty thick, and Ella Mae, J.B., Juanita and me, I guess we got lost. We kept going a little to the left and instead of hitting the fence where the road was, we hit the fence between Barkley's and us so we turned left and came back and hit another fence and wound up right down behind the barn at the tank. And we were there before we knew really where we were, but we finally got straightened out and across the field to the road and school.

Another thing that sticks in my mind about Busby, we were walking to school there and back. The Guelkers, Henry Guelker's boys, were probably a little more well-to-do than we were. They rode bicycles, and that always kind of stuck in our craws that those boys could ride bicycles, and we had to walk. We also had to take our lunch, and very seldom did we have paper sacks to carry our lunch in. Mother would wrap our lunch in a newspaper, and we'd have biscuits. And they'd get their lunch out of their brown paper bags with their white bread sandwiches, and we just always felt that was a little bit unfair.

They weren't too free to let us ride their bicycles, and one time we were coming home after it had snowed. Of course, us and Mac Walker's kids that lived down the road from us and two or three other families walked together, and we were always kind of buddies. Louella Walker was one of the older girls, and Doyn was the oldest boy because Carl Preston that day wasn't walking with us for some reason. But Mary Frances, Louella, Jack, Tooter, J.B., Ella Mae, Juanita and myself were all going from school, and we decided how fun it would be if we would hide under the bridge down there and build us up some snowballs. When the Guelker boys came by on their bicycles, we were gonna let them have it. Well, we did. We got ourselves a pretty good pile of snowballs built up, and here they came down the road. Henrunner Guelker, he was the oldest, was leading the

other two out. We jumped out and started hitting them with snowballs and, of course, Henrunner fell off his and bent a wheel. That made them mad so we got into a fight, and I don't remember who all was fighting who, but I know Henrunner jumped on me. He never did hit me, but he was bigger than I was, and he just got me down and sat on me. J.B. and Morris were fighting, and I think Tooter Walker and J.H. Guelker were into it. While we were fighting, Mary Frances—she was a pretty good-sized girl and she could cuss like a sailor—got their ink out of their baskets on their bicycles and poured it out in the snow. It'd make the prettiest circles and anyway we wound the fight up and started on home. They lived on down the road from where the fight had taken place, and their daddy came out and was gonna have them give us another whipping. This made Mary Frances pretty mad, and she jerked up an old sunflower out of bar-ditch. Of course, it being cold and snow on the ground, there was a clod of dirt about six inches around that came up with that old sunflower stalk, and it was about an inch in diameter. She got after Mr. Henry Guelker with that sunflower, and he took off for the house and she was telling him what for and lowering the boom on him and a cussing every step. She put him in the house, and I don't think the second fight ever came about. But we got along all right with the Guelker boys after that.

There's a lot of things happened at Busby. John and I were big enough and Ella Mae—she was kind of a tomboy, and I guess had rather play with us as Juanita—but she was always outside. We built us a trolley one time. We found some slick barbed wire which didn't have any barbs on it, and there was a big old mesquite tree on an earthen dam behind the barn. This dam was built up to catch the overflow from the horse trough. The cows a lot of times if the lot gate was shut would drink out of that little tank. Anyway, we tied our slick wire to the top of this old mesquite tree and then run it down to the corner of the cow lot. We lacked about three foot having enough wire to reach the corner but that's where we wanted to go to. We looked and looked and finally found some old rusty bailing wire. We found enough of that to splice onto our slick barbed wire and go to the corner, but we didn't think it would hold us. In fact, we were pretty sure it wouldn't hold us, but we kind of got our heads together and said Ella Mae is heavier than either one of us, and if we could get her to try it out for us and if it held her, it would hold us. Of course, on this wire we'd put about a two-foot length of pipe, three-quarter galvanized pipe, and our idea was to get a hold of this pipe, jump out of this tree and just slide this pipe down the wire to the ground. So we hollered at Eller, telling her what a good time we'd had sliding down that trolley, and that we wanted her to try it. Of course Eller being a little bit gullible, she just went right up that tree and we slung the pipe up to her and she bailed out and just as soon as her weight hit that rusty bailing wire broke and down she come, hit right on her tail-end and knocked the breath out of her. When she got her breath she's crying, telling us she was gonna go tell Mother so we just got a straddle of her, both of us, and we held her down until she promised she wouldn't tell Momma on us. And I don't think Eller's ever forgiven John and me, but we just had to do whatever was necessary to check that thing out because we didn't want to fall that far, and we thought Eller could take it better than we could.

Another thing I remember about Busby, Dad had an old mule that we called Tobe. And Tobe, I guess, was up in years. Every time you'd goose him, he couldn't keep from breaking wind. J.B. and I thought that was the funniest thing we'd ever heard in our lives to get old Tobe to break wind. The old fellow'd be in the lot, and if he ever laid down next to the fence we'd crawl on our hands and knees just as far as we had to slip up on him and goose him with a stick through the fence. He'd jump up and poot. We just thought that was the funniest thing we'd ever heard in our life.

Another time I remember Dad had maize in the maize crib and that's what he fed his horses to work them. Barkley's mules had been getting out and coming over there at night, and they'd break into the side door on the barn and eat maize. Well, he had bought some Highlife. Now we didn't know what Highlife was, but if you put it on an animal, it burned. He's gonna try to catch both these mules with their heads in the maize crib and pour Highlife down their back and see if he couldn't break them from coming over there. Well, when he explained to us what it was for, we got a bright idea. Mother had an old yellow tomcat she called Ol' Tom, and she thought he was the best mouser in the world. So we were out in the harness shed, and Ol' Tom he was rubbing on our legs and a purring, and we decided how funny it would be if we put some of this Highlife on his tail. Well, that's what we did, doused him up a little and put him down. He rubbed our leg and purred a little bit. Seems to me like it was a minute or so before that Highlife began to take effect, but when it hit him he took off for the house in a long run. He'd run about twenty steps then he'd just kick his back legs out from under him and drag his sitter on the ground. I guess that stuff was really burning, but he did that two or three times between the harness shed and the house. Mother and Dad were sitting under a big elm tree in back of the house, and we were peeping through the cracks of the harness shed and we thought that was sure funny. Ol' Tom went by dragging his sitter, and Mother said, "Press, you're gonna have to get some copper. That ol' cat's wormy." And we just had a fit, we thought that was real funny.

Several things we'd do to Eller. We would take the wheels off our red wagon when they wore the tires off and built us what we called a porter-car. We'd take some two-by-fours and get some nails and drive them in a two-by-four and bend them over the axle and put us a bolt through the front one where you put your feet on the front two-by-four that was crossways that had the wheels on it. That's the way you'd guide it. We'd drive it down the cellar door. Eller wanted a ride so we told her okay she could take a ride, and she got on and said where's the brakes. J.B. or I one, I don't remember which, said in order to stop it you had to reach back and grab those rear wheels and slide them. Well, she reached the bottom and reached back and grabbed the rear wheels and, of course, they ran over her fingers and cut one of them pretty bad. We always felt, or I did and I think John did too, pretty bad about that. Eller was always game for anything.

Another time I remember we was chopping cotton, I believe. I had to go to the house, me or J.B. one, I don't remember which, to get some water. Of course, Eller had her gum stuck under the kitchen table, and she wanted us to bring that gum back to her.

We got the gum and stuck our finger in it, made a little hole and filled it full of black pepper and carried it down just as innocent like. Eller got her gum and popped it in her mouth and went to chewing, and I don't think Eller likes black pepper to this day. I can see why, I guess.

We were always staying at the house on Saturday evenings while Mother and Dad went to Sweetwater to buy groceries. Any time they left, Eller, J.B. and I'd jump in the kitchen and make us some fudge. Mother bought her vanilla flavoring from the Watkins man, who also sold Watkins liniment in a bottle just about the same size and same color as the vanilla flavoring. We got a big dose of Watkins liniment in the fudge for flavoring and that wasn't too hot a fudge. I know we went out and buried it in the field and always laughed when Dad plowed, hoping he didn't get stuck in the fudge.

Another thing I remember about Carl Preston, Dad had an old Ford, probably a '33 model and Carl was old enough to be dating. He'd been out on a date the night before, and he's telling me and J.B. he had some trouble with the gear shift on the car and he wanted to show us what it was. The little cap that holds the gearshift down to the transmission, the little screw had come loose on it, and he took off in first gear and shifted to second and then he pulled the gearshift plumb out of the floorboard. Man, we didn't know whether we were gonna wreck or not. We didn't know what was going on, but now he really thought that was funny. Of course, he could just put it back in there and change second to third, but he gave J.B. and me a scare.

I'll never forget our trips back to Blackwell in the summer when school was out. J.B. and I would go back to Blackwell and stay with Myrt and Bill. Myrt had married while we were at Blackwell and didn't move to Busby with us. We had some fun hunting wasp nests on the creek with Myrt. We'd go down and spend a couple weeks and man we'd get our pockets full of rocks to shoot those big black wasp nests down and then just run like scared rabbits to try to keep them from stinging us. That was more fun than you would think.

I also remember going with Arnold to run trap lines. I always thought I learned a lot from Arnold about wildlife. I just thought he knew all there was to know about it. I know he would set these traps, and he was hunting ring-tailed cats, coons and whatever he could catch. I never could figure out why he'd take the cigarette package and take the foil and put over the trigger of the trap and put it in the edge of the water. He was the one that told me a coon's curiosity would always get the best of him. He'd see something shining in the water, and he'd have to get down there and feel of it with his paw to see what it was. I thought that was amazing to take something like the foil off a cigarette wrapper and put on a steel trap for bait. I know one time he and Mildred lived south of Blackwell, and I think it was on their granddaddy's place, but we found a pretty good size nest in a tree, and it had white birds in it, pretty good size birds. J.B. and I couldn't figure out what they were, and Arnold told us that was a buzzard nest. You know a buzzard is just as black as the ace of spades, but their young ones are white. He's the one that taught me about the trap lines, how to bait a trap, a little buzzard was white, and I always enjoyed going down there and running his trap line with him.

Sometime after that in the winter, J.B. and I got to thinking we were pretty good hunters. I know it had come a shower, and we were up in the pasture north of the house behind the barn a hunting, and there was an old skunk that had run in a bush. We're trying to get it out where we could shoot it. I think we just had our slingshots, and I finally told John if he'd take that short stick and crawl up there and punch that skunk when he came out I'd shoot him. Well, John got up there pretty close. If I remember, the stick wasn't but about three feet long, and when John punched that skunk, he sprayed him good. I tell you I had a time getting him home. When we got to the house, Mother and Dad and the rest of the kids were sitting down at the supper table to eat. That smell was bad, and J.B. got sick. I know we had to carry him to the horse trough and pull his clothes off and give him a bath, and we finally got him cleaned up enough that we could get him in the house. I don't know whether we ever ate that night or not, I can't remember.

Dad had an old black mare that we called Shine. J.B. and I'd ride her a whole lot, and she's just as gentle as she could be, but one time we were coming from the tank up to the barn and old Shine was standing there with her head over the gate and one rear foot cocked up. I guess she was asleep. I walked right up behind her and slapped her on the rump, and said "Hi, Shine, ol' kid." When I did, she kicked me right in the stomach. I'll never forget how sick I was all night long. But I always respected a horse after that and never walked right up behind one.

Another time I remember us walking to school, and we went over the hill and saw something laying in the road. We couldn't figure out what it was, and it was a dead mule, one of Barkley's mules. Come to find out Rake Carlton, he owned the store at Busby, was coming in from Sweetwater with his Model A and his groceries. He always drove pretty fast anyway, but he'd hit that old mule and killed it. We thought that was funny, him running over Barkley's mule.

While we lived at Busby, *[cousins]* Clint and Jake Lewis came to visit us a few times. Clint we called "Bub." He and Jake never could get along too well. I remember one time the tank down below the house had frozen over. It was in the winter time and left a pretty thick ice on it when Uncle Clyde, Aunt Ione, Clint and Bub came to see us. Carl and Jake and Bub and myself and J.B. decided we'd go on to the tank and play ice hockey. I think we called it shinney at the time, ice shinney, but we'd take a tin can and get us an old mesquite limb about the size of a baseball bat and we'd throw this tin can on the ice and try to knock it across the other one's goal line. Carl and Jake teamed up against Bub, myself and John and they was beating us pretty bad. Bub got kinda mad about it. I know they had knocked the can across our goal line and had turned around and were skating back to the other end of the tank. Bub took his mesquite limb and threw it on the ice, and it just went to spinning end around end, you know, and hit Jake right on the heels and just knocked him up in the air. His head was the first thing to hit the ground and that broke up the ice shinney game.

Another thing I remember about Bub, I was going to school in Sweetwater and had just begun to kinda notice the girls. I spent the night with Bub, and he was gonna introduce his country cousin with the night life of Sweetwater. He was gonna show me how to pick up girls. Bub had an old Model T that I guess uncle Clyde had bought for him, but he drove this Model T. I know we got all shined up, and he was gonna show his country cousin how it was done. We left where they lived on Ninth Street and went up to Oak or one of those streets and turned toward town where there were two little girls walking up the sidewalk. He said, "Now let me show you how it is done," so he pulled over and stopped. He said "Hi, girls, how about going for a ride with us?" And one of them said, "You got any gas?" And he said, "Yeah, I got a tankful." They said, "Well then, crank up and go to hell." I thought it was funny, but Bub didn't think it was a bit funny, but if I remember right we went back to the house, and that was the last lesson I got from him on how to pick up girls.

Mother got sick when I was going to high school in Sweetwater. I decided I had to quit school and help Dad farm. Somebody had to stay with her pretty often, you know, stay close so I just thought I had to quit school and help Dad farm. I did that for about a year, I guess, then decided I needed to find me an occupation. I can remember my greatest desire was to get a job making $200 a month, $50 a week. I thought if I could do that for about ten years I would just retire as rich as I could be, so I saw an ad in the paper about a sheet metal school in Dallas. I called or wrote a letter and enrolled, and I remember Johnnie Ammons carrying me to Dallas. I stayed with my Aunt Ethel and Uncle Claude Southwood out at Victory. I rode the interurban from Victory to Dallas to go to school. If I remember right, it was about a three-month school, and they guaranteed me a job after I finished. After I finished, they did get me a job with Southern Aircraft out at Garland. By that time the war had broken out and Southern Aircraft had a contract with the government to build tail turrets for the B-24 bomber. So I stayed with them for a year, year and a half, and worked and had a lot of fun while I was there.

Uncle Claude Southwood was a painter and his only boy Tug was about five years younger than me. Tug and I ran around and had a lot of fun, but Claude he kind of liked his beer and his whiskey. I never will forget he'd cut his paint with turpentine to thin it. He'd empty his turpentine bottles, and he'd take his whiskey then and wash the turpentine bottles out and pour his whiskey in his turpentine bottles and set them on the shelves in his garage so Aunt Ethel wouldn't find them. Tug and I used to hide out behind the shed and watch him go to the garage. He'd get him a turpentine bottle, and he'd take him a little nip. He painted with Noal Tony, his son-in-law, who was Gladys' husband, and Gladys didn't know that Tony drank as much as he did, I don't think, but both him and Uncle Claude would go to that garage pretty regular and get them a little nip out of that turpentine bottle. Me and Tug thought that was funny to watch them do that.

Soon after I went to work, I got enough money saved up to buy me a '36 Ford. It was a two-door, dark blue with red wheels. I thought that Ford was just about the greatest thing in the world. I hadn't had it too long until I had trouble with it losing water. I figured out it had a blown head gasket so the Loveless boys who ran a garage in Victory overhauled my engine and painted that thing for $30. I still didn't have but $140 or something like that in it and had a pretty good automobile.

Maxine's oldest sister was married to Uncle Claude's oldest nephew, who was Crave Southwood. While I was living with Aunt Ethel, Ruby and Crave brought Maxine and Mildred over one Sunday evening and was visiting with Aunt Ethel and Uncle Claude. Tug and I were down at the swimming pool, and they sent someone down and wanted us to come home and that's when I first met Maxine. I always thought Aunt Ethel was trying to make a match there because she asked Maxine and Mildred if they'd go in and set supper on the table for Tug and me. Seems as though the rest of them had eaten, but Tug and I hadn't. So after we had eaten a bite, she suggested—Aunt Ethel did—that Tug and I carry Maxine and Mildred to the show. I guess that was Maxine's and my first date, and we dated after that for a year or two until we got married on January 11, 1944.

While I was working at Southern Aircraft, I got to be pretty good buddies with three more boys that worked out there by the names of Thomas George, Ben Humphreys and Ed Hutchens. We decided that we needed to get us an apartment in Dallas because we were working nights, so we did. We rented us a two-room apartment on Gaston Avenue in Dallas and the four of us lived together in that apartment and got along real well and worked until I went into the service.

We were working the evening shift at Southern, and we'd nearly always come in on Skillman Avenue. There we'd stop at a little cafe and eat before we came home. We were working from about three to eleven if I remember right. We'd eat us a bite and then go on home. Well, I had the '36 Ford and Ed Hutchins had a Chevrolet. He had about a '39 Chevrolet; it was a little newer car than mine, but Ben and I for some reason one night had driven together and Ed Hutchins and Tommy George had ridden together in Ed's car. Well, I had put twin exhausts on mine—it was pretty loud—and after we ate Ed said something about we'll beat you home so Ben and I jumped in that Ford and we took off down Gaston Avenue and had the hammer down pretty good. Directly Ben said, "You'd better slow down. There's a cop right up here on this side street." Well, I was done going above the speed limit so I just went ahead. Of course, they just pulled out behind us. We went over a little rise and I thought well we had to give them the slip and I shut my headlights off and made a right-hand turn on Bryan Parkway. I went down about three or four blocks and made a left, still with my lights off. We saw the cops, they didn't take that last left, and they went on by with their red lights on. We were laughing about how we'd given them the slip, but the street we were on made a gradual turn to the right.

The next thing I knew, we'd jumped the curb, and we'd run this '36 Ford right up into an old man's house. His bedroom was on front, and he had his bed cattycorner across one of the front corners and we hit that corner of the house. There wasn't anything but the deck lid showing on that '36 Ford, but it kinda knocked me out. When I came to, I couldn't find Ben; he was out of the car, but I could hear the old gentleman sitting over there on the floor and he's saying, "What in the world happened? What in the world happened?" But he got the light on, and he had on his long-handled underwear. Well, I finally came to and got out and probably didn't make any sense to him at all. But some women from across the street came over and got me on a couch, they had an icepack on my head. That was quite an experience.

Now I believe we called Ed and Thomas, and they came back and picked us up and carried us home. The cops never did catch us, but the next morning I took off from work and went over to see the old man. He's pretty mad as it'd torn his house up pretty good. He had my car with a chain around it running through another door and chained to something, I think the kitchen stove. He wasn't going to let me move my car until I fixed his house. I ran out to Victory and got Uncle Claude and Tony. They came back with me to talk to him; and we finally agreed that we'd patch his house up and re-paper two rooms; and they painted it; and we came out of it all right. You know jug-headed boys will do some funny things, and I never could figure out later on why I had my lights out and was running from the cops. I should've just paid my fine and taken my medicine. But anyway, that's the way it happened, but I've always thought I was a little more careful driver after that.

Mother's daddy, Doc Garrett, my grandfather, was still living when I was in Victory. He lived in Plano. Mother had a younger brother, Uncle Fred, and he lived in Norman, Oklahoma, for a while. I think grandpa was staying in Plano with Aunt Bird or somebody along about that time when her brother Uncle Fred would visit. I'd go to Plano quite often and see them and visit with Grandpa Garrett. I remember one time Uncle Fred came to Aunt Ethel's, and he wanted me to carry him to Oklahoma, so one Saturday evening late he and I took off north up *[Highway]* 75 to Oklahoma. We got just inside Oklahoma and I believe it was at Ada, but there was a cafe there he wanted me to stop and went in. He ordered me a steak, and I didn't see him for about thirty or forty minutes. I couldn't figure out what really was going on, but directly he came back and he said he was ready to go back to Plano, so we headed back. I did this two or three times, and he always went to this one particular café but I never knew why. I found out later. One morning I got up, and I saw him in the turtle of my car. He was unloading a couple cases of whiskey and unbeknownst to me I was carrying him up there to get whiskey and he was bringing it back to Plano. I decided probably we'd better stop our trips to Oklahoma after that. I think he'd bring it back to Uncle Charley's café. Charley Mayes was

Aunt Bird's husband, and he ran a cafe there in Plano. Now I don't know what they had going, but I kind of found myself right in the middle, and I stopped those trips to Oklahoma.

(Shortly after ending his trips to Oklahoma, Ray realized he was going to be drafted so he volunteered for the Army. Before going to the European Theater with the 552nd AAA Battalion, he married Maxine Staton on January 11, 1944. He landed on Normandy and fought through the end of the war in Europe before returning home. As he concludes his recollections, he speaks of his "two" families: his natural family and his Army family, the 552nd. From 1951 until his death, he attended the annual Lewis Reunion. From 1972 until his demise, he also participated in the annual get-togethers of the 552nd.)

I've said a lot of times I'm somewhat proud to have spent the time in the service that I did. I guess if it was a necessity and I had to, I'd do it again, but I certainly wouldn't be as enthusiastic as I first went in before.

After our discharge, I worked in Dallas for a while and contacted two or three of the *[army]* boys and had contact with them at different times the first two or three years, but soon lost all contact with them. In the middle of November after I was discharged, Maxine and I decided to go on our honeymoon before I went to work. Not having a car, Dad was good enough to let me use the '39 Dodge he had. Maxine and I went to Montgomery, Alabama. Ralph *[his brother-in-law]* was stationed at Maxwell Field there, and Marie was living at Wetumpka. Karyl had been born, and I'd never seen Karyl. We visited the family. It was good to see the kiddos that was born while I was overseas and had not seen before. Maxine and I took off to Montgomery, Alabama, and just had a wonderful time. The best I remember we were gone a couple weeks, something like that, but I never will forget the first night we went into Marie and Ralph's house in Wetumpka. Of course, Reatha I had seen before I'd left. She was just as cute as a speckled pup. We walked in that night and Ralph and Marie and the girls were sitting at the supper table and Reatha still looked like a little doll, but Karyl was just a little over a year old, and her hair was kind of stringy. What made it worse was she had mashed potatoes and gravy in front of her. Evidently, she was getting tired and sleepy because she'd rubbed potatoes on her face and in her hair; and that made it a little stickier. Not taking anything away from Karyl, she was a cute little girl, but I thought my goodness what's wrong with her with that stringy hair and potatoes all over her, but we really enjoyed our visit out there. Reatha had a couple little Negro friends and their names were Junior and Virginia, but Reatha called them Bejunior and Beginia, and she had to introduce us to them, and we just had a good time. Coming home we went down the coastline to Mobile and on down to Beaumont and spent the night with Uncle George *[Lewis]* and Aunt Sue. They lived in Beaumont at that time. I remember that Aunt Sue and Uncle George had been goose hunting, and she had baked goose for supper one night. I never was too fond of duck or goose, but that tasted pretty well.

We got on back home and bought us an automobile and I worked in Dallas for a while at different things. Never was too successful at any of them. Finally, we moved back to Sweetwater, farmed a little bit, dairied a little bit. We had three kiddos, Carl, of course, then Jerry and Vicki. After being in the dairy business for a while—the drought in the early '50s made that almost impossible—I hired out to Lone Star Cement at Maryneal and worked for them for about nine years, and then I decided I wasn't moving as fast as I thought my capabilities— and I had very few of them—but I thought I could do better with another company, so I went to work for Texas Industries in Midlothian, Tex., and that's where I retired.

The kiddos all grew up and got married, and I tell everybody we've got a full house in grandkids, three jacks and a pair of queens, and I wouldn't take anything for any of them, but probably wouldn't give fifteen cents for another one.

Sometime in the early '70s, probably '71 we began to get correspondence from one Troy Thomason, who lived at Groesbeck, Texas. He was in the 552nd headquarters battery and was real interested in contacting everyone he had an address for and trying to organize a reunion for the 552nd. Well, this just set me on fire. It's hard for me to explain, but when you're with twenty-two boys for about thirty-two months, eat and sleep and depend on one another, you get fairly close. I really feel that this group of boys was as good a group as any group its size in the service. I think we looked out for one another. There's no doubt in my mind there was several things happened that had it not been for some of the boys on the crew, I wouldn't be sitting here at the kitchen table tonight.

So I was real enthused to begin to get correspondence from someone in the unit who wanted to put a reunion together. This came about on July 2, 1972, in Waco, Texas.

The 552nd was made up primarily—85 percent I'd say—from Texas and Oklahoma. The other 15 percent being a few from California, the balance from Maine, New Hampshire, Massachusetts, New York, New Jersey and the Northeast area. The date was set for our first reunion, and I was working at Texas Industries in Midlothian at the time. Maxine and I got loaded up and headed for Waco, and I would just think about things that had happened during the war on the trip to Waco and wonder if I was gonna recognize any of them. It'd been almost twenty-seven, lacking from July 2nd to November 2nd being twenty-seven years since I'd seen any of them. I know that the first night after meeting a few of them and not recognizing many I got nervous, but the longer I looked at them the more things began to come back to me. I was so nervous I got sick at my stomach. I spent the balance of the night going from the bed to the bathroom, but I think it was nothing more than the excitement and thinking about things that had happened had left me all keyed up. So anyway I made it through the night, and we've had a reunion every two years since 1972, a battalion reunion, and on the odd years since we've had a battery reunion. I just would not take anything for the enjoyment that we've gotten out of getting together with these people in the last twelve years. I think Maxine would tell you the same thing. The women seem to enjoy it as much as the men, maybe now a little more. They've made good friends, and it's just a lot of pleasure to make these reunions. Of course at every one we fight the same battles; we fight the same war; and it comes out the same every time. Someone will think of something new that someone hasn't remembered had happened, and there's a lot of argument about how it happened, I guess that's a sign of getting old, but we'll finally thrash it around and come to some decision that it happened this away. This has been absolutely great to get together with these guys for the last twelve years.

I'm gonna say in closing this thing up that, the only thing I derive more pleasure, more enjoyment out of than these meetings with the boys I was in the service with, is our family reunions. I just love for this time of year to come around. I'm so proud the Lewises get along as well as they do together. I think we're a close family. I think there's a lot of love in the family. I don't think it, I know it. It just does me a lot of good to get together with my brother and sisters and all their kids at this time of year, and I am especially looking forward to this coming weekend. We always have a good time, and I'm just so thankful that our family gets along and enjoys getting together like we do. I'm sure you know a lot of families are not as close as we are. I just can't understand people that don't enjoy the get-togethers of their family. I'm sure we've been fortunate, and I'm thankful for that. I just hope we continue as long as we're still able to have these get-togethers somewhere and have this fellowship that we do at these reunions.

Ray Franklin Lewis
De Leon, Texas
1984

CHAPTER EIGHT

John Bracken Lewis

I was born June 15, 1926, near Roscoe, Texas. The farm I was born on was known as the Forrester place because the landowner was named Forrester. The Forrester place was the second place the family lived after moving from East Texas. Dad worked it on the halves, which meant the landowner furnished all the farm equipment and Dad got half the farm production. From then on, he bought horses and equipment and paid one third of the feed and one fourth of the cotton.

I lived here until I was possibly three or four years old. I have very little recollection of things that happened on this place. One thing I do remember is we were going to the cellar one night as we did every time there was a bad cloud coming up. I remember trying to get to the cellar, and the strong wind blew me off down towards the barn off about fifty or sixty yards from the cellar, and my dad had to come down there and get me. That scared me a lot worse than the storm. I do remember getting to go to the cotton gin with my dad for the first time when we lived on this place. We had horses hooked to the wagon with *[the equivalent of]* a bale of cotton on the wagon with high sideboards. It seemed to me it was ten or twelve feet from the top of the wagon down to the horses, and you looked down on top of the horses. I'm sure it wasn't that high, but to me that's the way it seemed.

The next place I remember living was known as the Younger place, again being so-called because the landowner was named Younger. It was at this place that I remember burying a jar of marbles in the backyard. I don't really remember why I buried them, but it was real clear in my mind that I thought that would be the safest thing to do with them. I really don't remember whether I dug them back up or not. I'm sure that I possibly did.

The next place we lived was known as the Woodard place. We must have moved there in 1931 or '32. This house we lived in there had an upstairs, and I remember one night getting up in the middle of the night to go outside to use the bathroom. We had to go down the stairs, and the stairs opened out on to the front porch. And, somehow or another, I stumbled and fell down the stairs through the door on the outside and ended up in the snow out in the front yard. One of my older sisters—I believe it was Myrt—came down and got me and brought me back to bed.

I remember this old house had a fireplace which was actually the only source of heat we had except for the wood cook stove in the kitchen. I remember it was real cold that winter we lived there, and I remember backing up to the fireplace trying to stay warm. I also remember that Mother would cook biscuits in the fireplace. She would take a Dutch oven and rake some coals out and put coals under the oven and on top and put our biscuits in and bake them that way.

It was also on this place that I started to school. The first school I attended was known as Brownlee, which was a little country school about three or four miles from where we lived. We would walk through the pasture to school. It was on this place that I became old enough to pick cotton, and this is my first recollection of cotton-picking. The first car I remember my Dad having was on this place. I believe it was a 1923 Dodge. When we all went somewhere, I had to sit on a gallon bucket on the back floorboard. I remember coming home from town one night in fairly cold weather, and the old car didn't have any windows on the doors, just curtains. I don't believe they were even on at that time because I remember freezing to death sitting in the back before we got home.

The old farmhouse that we lived in at that time was not very good. I remember the paper on the inside was just a duff-colored wallpaper, and it was held on with nails and little round pieces of tin about the size of a quarter. These were on the inside of the house and nailed through the tin into the wood to hold the wallpaper on. When the wind blew you could see the paper move some from the wind coming in and out through the wall.

The old Brownlee school building is still standing today. It is used as a community center for the people in that area. I only went to school at Brownlee the first half of my first year in school. Along in January we moved to Blackwell, and I finished up the second half of my first year in the school in Blackwell.

The place we lived on there had a creek running through it, and I have a lot of pleasant memories of all the fun we had playing and swimming on this creek. I remember one time, evidently in about 1933, when it was sort of dry down there. Dad's cattle watered in the creek. It got so dry that most of the water dried up, and Dad went down in the middle of the creek bed and dug a well about four feet across and ten or twelve feet deep down to water. We would draw water out of there with a bucket and a rope and pour it in a tub for the cows to water. I remember one time we went down there to draw water for the cows. We looked down in the bottom, and there was one of our cows that had fallen in the well. I don't remember just exactly how Dad got it out, but I do know that it was quite a chore to get the cow out of the well.

The first I remember of doing any kind of fishing was on this place. We used to take pins and make us fish hooks, go down to the creek and dig some worms and catch some perch out of this creek. I also remember one day that Ella Mae and Ray and myself were going to go to the creek and cook our lunch. We carried some bacon and eggs, and I was probably seven or eight years old at the time. We got over there and couldn't get a fire started. So, they talked me into going back to the house and bringing some coal oil so they could start a fire. We got our fire started, and Ella Mae was going to boil some eggs for our lunch. I remember she got the water boiling and put the eggs in there and evidently just left them a few minutes because when we tried to eat them they were almost raw.

Also the first hunting of any kind I remember was on this place. Dad and some of his brothers used to go squirrel hunting there a lot, as there were quite a few squirrels on the creek. I would go with them. As they would kill the squirrels, I would carry them. I would have two or three in each hand. After you would carry them a little way, the hair on their tails would come out, and they would be hard to hold. Their tails would be slick as they could be, and their heads would drag on the ground no bigger than I was at that time.

The first school bus we ever rode was when we lived in Blackwell. I remember one morning we got on the school bus, and we were about the last ones to get on. Maybe there was two or three families to get on after we did. When I got on the bus I happened to stand close to the door, and when the bus driver closed the door, I had my finger on the door, and he closed the door on my finger. I was too timid to say anything about it, so I suffered about a half a mile down the road to the next bus stop until he opened the door to let on some more kids, and I got my finger out of the door.

I remember at Blackwell school the railroad came within about a hundred yards of the school building. For some reason the track was cut down into the ground, and it was about six or eight feet below ground level. Some of the older boys, I remember, when they got ready to play hooky would work their way out close to the railroad track, and when the teacher wasn't looking, they would hop in this railroad cut and take off down the railroad track to the creek and play hooky.

Ray and I had so much fun playing on the creek at Blackwell. In the summertime we took baths in the creek. Ray and I made us a swing across the creek. We tied a rope to a limb on a big tree that hung over the creek with a stick tied to the bottom of the rope. We would hold the stick with both hands and swing across the creek. That was a lot of fun until one day I decided to do it with one hand. Ella Mae tried to talk me out of it, but I was going to prove that I could. Ray told me he could hold on with one hand and swing across, which he did. I tried it with one hand behind me to prove that I did it with one hand. Well, I got out across the middle of the creek, lost my grip and fell to the dry creek bed and broke my left arm. That is actually the first time I remember going to the doctor to have my arm set.

The first Christmas I remember was on the farm at Roscoe. The old farm house had a fireplace and Mother and Dad hung socks on the mantle with fruits and nuts in them for us kids—no toys. The first *real* Christmas I remember was at Blackwell. It was evidently the Christmas of 1933 because some of the older girls, Marie and Mildred, had gone to Sweetwater or Roscoe—I don't remember for sure which—and were working. They bought us some toys for Christmas, which were actually the first real toys I remember getting for Christmas. It seemed like all the time before that we got mostly candy and fruit and things to eat or clothes to wear. At this time our older sisters bought Ray and me a couple little trucks. I remember the trucks had little flashlight batteries in them and headlights on the front of them that would actually burn. We got under the bed in one of the bedrooms and played with these trucks with the headlights on. That was also the year we got our first little red wagon, and we were all three of us, Ray, Ella Mae and myself, going to ride in this wagon down the hill there at Blackwell. Well, we all three got in and started down the hill, and I don't remember for sure who was driving, but whoever was driving ran us into a tree and knocked the front wheels out from under our wagon the first day we had it. In fact, it was on Christmas Day as I recall.

I remember one time we were going fishing over at another place. In fact, it was on another creek about seven or eight miles from where we lived. At that time Dad had an old 1926 model Dodge with the batteries under the floorboards instead of under the hood like they are today. So in order to take the battery out of the car you had to take the floorboard up to get to the battery. Anyway, we were driving out through this pasture, and Dad hit a stump. Evidently, this battery hung down a little low under the car, and I remember it knocked the battery plumb out of the car. We had to walk back, and it seemed like we got a wagon and team and came back over there and pulled the old car back home.

I remember when we lived in Blackwell one Sunday afternoon we were playing ball out in the pasture out in front of the house, and my older brother Carl Preston stepped on what we called a pincushion or a devil's cushion as some people call it. It is an odd cactus that grows almost flat on the ground, and these things have real sharp thorns on them with barbs on the thorns. He stuck one of these things in his foot and at that time, of course, you didn't think too much about going to the doctor. I remember that Dad took his knife and cut this thing out of my brother's foot. Seems like two or three of the older girls had to hold him while Dad cut it out of his foot. I know it made a big enough impression on me of the pain he went through that I sure did watch out for those things from then on.

One thing I remember about the old houses we lived in when we were kids is I never remember having a living room. It was all bedrooms and kitchen. What we called the front bedroom was used as a living room when we had company on Sunday. The people sat on the bed and, of course, we moved chairs in and made a temporary living room out of our front bedroom.

Another thing I remember we used to do for entertainment when we lived in Blackwell is we would build slingshots, go down to the creek and shoot down wasp nests. A lot of times we would find nests as big as your hand, and the thrill of it was to shoot the wasp nest down and then run before the wasps got to you and stung you.

In the fall of 1934 we moved to a little community called Busby. It was about ten or twelve miles north of Sweetwater. At the time I was in the third grade. Busby was a smaller school actually than Blackwell. The schoolhouse had four rooms, first, second and third grade in one room with one teacher; fourth, fifth and sixth in another room with one teacher; and the same with the other two rooms. The teacher would teach the first grade class a lesson; then she would teach the second grade class; and then she would teach the third grade a lesson. If your class wasn't having a lesson, you studied while the other classes were having their lessons. There was no electricity so it was heated by coal with big stoves in each room. Me and the boys loved to go get coal just to get out of the classroom.

The schoolhouse had two outdoor toilets, boys and girls. They were about forty or fifty yards from the school because of the smell. The drinking water was rainwater that ran from the gutter on the building to a cistern. The cistern had a hand pump that put water to about four faucets. Someone had to pump while the kids were drinking. The boys would love to quit pumping when the girls were drinking.

We walked three miles to school as there were no buses at Busby. One time there at Busby—it was in the winter—we had to walk to school. We got up that morning, and it was real foggy. You couldn't see but about thirty feet in front of you. Me, Ray and Ella Mae started to school, and we were going to cut across the field to the road and save some time. We got out in this field and evidently just walked in a big circle because we walked about twenty or thirty minutes and walked up behind a barn. The barn looked awfully familiar. After we got up pretty close, we realized it was our own barn. We'd made a circle and come back to the house.

A lot of times in the fall of the year when school started, we wouldn't begin school because we'd have to pick cotton. The school year was only eight months and sometimes [school] was closed six to eight weeks during cotton-picking time so the kids could pick cotton. In fact, sometimes there were enough kids out of school picking cotton that they would just turn school out in the main part of the cotton-picking season. This time was not made up, so sometimes we only had six months of school.

When I was in the fifth through the seventh grade, we played basketball on the dirt court. I remember getting hit on the left side of my head with the ball. I don't remember that I knew it was [coming] because I could not see out of my left eye. We played all sports on a dirt court. In a radius of about eight miles from Busby, there were eight country schools: Moody, Claytonville, Capitola, Longworth, Palava, Barrenview and Center that we played sports against. We were playing at Highland School one time, and when you went in to replace someone you ran by the ref and told him who you were replacing, then he would holler whoever's name it was and "off." We had a kid named Jack Walker. Someone went in to replace him, and when the ref yelled the change, it almost broke up the game as we could not quit laughing. By the way, the ref was Ralph Ammons.

At Busby in the summer time people had parties in their home. Kids anywhere from twelve to eighteen years old would attend. One game I liked was called "knock and go strolling." The girls would be in the house and the boys outside. The girls had numbers that the boys did not know. The boys would knock on the door and call a number, and that girl would come out and go walking with him. Us boys were always trying to get the number of the girl that we wanted to walk with.

It was along about this time I remember the first bought bread I ever ate. It came in a loaf just about like it does today, only it wasn't sliced. You had to take it home and slice it yourself. And also that is about the first time I remember having bologna to eat. We thought it was a real treat on Saturday night if we had bologna for our Saturday night meal.

We didn't have electricity at that time, and I remember studying by an old coal oil lamp. In fact, my mother cooked on a coal oil cook stove. We had a barrel of coal oil—actually it was mostly known as kerosene—and we had to go out with a coal oil bucket and bring coal oil in for the cook stove. Many times I had to go get a bucket of kerosene from that outside barrel for her cooking.

My mother never lived in a house with running water. It was creek and windmill [water] at Blackwell. At Busby it was rain and hauled water. The Busby house was guttered with a cistern, which was a hole dug in the ground about twenty-five feet deep and five feet wide with concrete walls and bottom. Rainwater ran off the house into the cistern. There was a wood rack above the cistern and a pulley with rope and bucket to draw the water out. It was deep enough that the water was cool in the summer. That is what we used for drinking water [at Busby]. Every so often it needed cleaning, and Dad would lower me down to the bottom on a rope to clean it up. I would put the dirty water in a bucket, and he would pull it up and dump it. We had a windmill over a well [at Busby], but the water was gyppy or salty. It was used for horses and cows to drink. I can remember many times mother said, "Son, go draw a bucket of water."

There was a round metal tank that the windmill pumped into. It was about six-feet wide and three-feet deep. In the summer we took a bath in it. Also, there was a dam in the pasture that made a tank. The boys swam in it in the summer. Also, ducks came to it in the winter. I remember when I was twelve or thirteen years old and saw ducks on it, Mother let me take the old 12-gauge shotgun. I made a circle down in the field, crawled up behind the dam and shot at a duck. The gun kicked so hard that it knocked me back down the dam. I did not know that I killed the duck until I crawled back up the dam, but I did. My mother was so glad to cook the duck for lunch.

I recall coming home from school a lot of afternoons when we lived in Busby and looking in the oven. Mother would leave the biscuits left over from lunch in the oven, and we would have cold biscuits, butter and syrup.

I can remember a few times on Sunday afternoon we decided to make a freezer of ice cream. Of course, we would have to go to town to get ice if we didn't have enough in our icebox, which ordinarily we didn't have. While someone went to town to get ice to freeze the cream, someone would go to the pasture and milk the cows to get enough milk to make the ice cream. You couldn't buy crushed ice at that time; it was all block ice. I remember we would take a cotton sack, put this block of ice in the sack, take the ax and beat it up so we would have crushed ice to put in the ice cream freezer. There were no phones, and sometime Dad's brothers or sisters and their families would just come to see us on Sunday afternoons. One Sunday in Busby we made a freezer of ice cream, but when we got it made, we saw Uncle Clint's family coming down the road. We took the freezer to the barn and hid it until they left.

In the hot summer us boys would sleep outside with a quilt on the ground. I joined the Liberty Baptist Church at Busby around 1938 or 1939 and was baptized in John Ammons's tank.

The way my dad rented these places we lived on was what they called thirds and fourths. What that meant was that he would pay a third of all the feed that he had raised to the landowner, and he would pay a fourth of all the cotton that he raised to the landowner. With this method, he furnished all his own farm equipment and so forth. There were some people who farmed on what they called the halves. The landowner would furnish the horses, the equipment and the land, and the tenant just raised the cotton and furnished the labor, but he would pay half of everything he raised to the landowner.

I remember after my parents would finish a crop, Dad and Mother would be talking, and the best I remember, if they made enough money to pay off all their debts or he could borrow enough money to make the next crop, they felt like they had had a pretty good year. I guess that was one of the reasons that one of our neighbors later told me—in fact, it was Jack Whitworth, Joe's brother—that I told him one time when I was probably ten or thirteen years old that I didn't know what I was going to be when I grew up, but one thing for sure, I was not going to be a cotton farmer.

I remember as a kid going to school I had to wear overalls and blue denim shirts. I sure did want to wear trousers or what we called "waistbands," but Mother and Dad seemed to think that overalls were much more practical because you could work in them whenever they got a little bit ragged or too ragged to wear to school. I was probably in the eighth grade before I was allowed to wear anything but overalls to school. I don't ever remember having a suit of clothes when I was a child. The first suit I remember, I bought it myself after I got out of the Merchant Marines.

As a kid I enjoyed building things. I would take an old apple box or anything I could find and any kind of wheels I could find and put the wheels on something and make what we called a porter-car. You would take a two-by-four and bore a hole right in the middle of it for a front axle and put a bolt from it up to the main part of the body where you could sit on it and put your feet on this two-by-four and turn your wheels left or right. I remember a lot of times Ray and I would take this thing whenever we were hauling in feed from out in the field with a wagon and the horses and mules, and we would tie our porter-car to the back of the wagon and ride this thing to the field and back.

I also remember taking bottles and using them as horses. There was a certain kind of a hair oil bottle—I believe it was a rose hair oil bottle—that I used to save. They were sort of square and I would put two of them together and take string and make my harness for my horses. I would use these bottles as horses, and I would build little old plows and so forth to hook these horses to and play in the sand. I also remember that Mother had a potato masher—a hand potato masher—which she would let me play with some because it made a good harrow. I would put a bottle on each side of the handle of this potato masher and get outside and play in the sand with it.

Way back when I was a boy we didn't even have an icebox. I remember on the weekend sometime Dad would buy ice, but we would wrap it in sacks and try to keep it through the weekend to drink iced tea with. The first icebox I remember having was at Busby, and we evidently got it in 1935 or '36. It was the old wooden type of icebox, and at that time there was an ice route. A man would come from Sweetwater about two or three times a week and deliver ice. You just opened the top of this icebox and put ice in the top of it. You kept your vegetables and your milk and stuff in the bottom. I remember that Mother would make us be real careful with the ice. We weren't allowed to chip ice off for our drinking water. We kept a jug of water sitting there on top of the ice and that's where we got our cool water to drink. And also in the cistern, that I mentioned earlier, the dug well that was plastered with cement and the rainwater ran off the house in there. That water was fairly cool when you would draw it out of the bottom as it was deep enough that the water was pleasantly cool to drink. Mother had what they called a window cooler, which was just a screened-in box with a canvas around the outside of it protruding from one of the windows. She would wet this canvas, and it would act somewhat like an evaporative air conditioner. It would keep the milk and butter and stuff cooler than in the kitchen.

I remember in 1932 when we lived on the Woodard place, Dad raised some wheat. I remember Mother cooking this wheat. She would just boil it in water, and we would eat it in the morning for breakfast as a cereal. The best I remember it was sort of spongy and chewy as you would eat it.

When we would go to work in the fields, we would carry a water jug, which was just a small-mouthed gallon glass jug, and we would wrap it in a burlap sack, wet this sack and set it in the shade. That would keep the water cool.

As I said before, Dad farmed with horses. I remember two or three colts when they got big enough that Ray and I would break them to ride and break them to work. I remember even when we were younger, we had a couple calves that we actually broke to work. We had one apiece, and we could ride them almost like we could ride a horse. We had them trained where we could just get on them, take a little stick, and tap them on one side of the neck or the other, and make them go where we wanted to.

The first bought cookies I ever remember were fig bars; seems like they were at a neighbor's house, a Mr. Mosely. I'm not sure just exactly what place we lived on at that time, but I wasn't but seven or eight years old, the best I remember.

The first radio I remember was at Uncle Cliff's house, and he lived in Sweetwater at the time. I remember Mother and Dad and the other children and myself would go down there on Saturday night and listen to the Grand Ole Opry. Also the first radio I remember in a car, Uncle Cliff had it, and it was in a 1936 Ford. I remember sometimes he would come up to the house. In fact, I remember one time he came up to the house, and we listened to all the prize fights. I'm not sure just exactly who it was, but I think it was Joe Louis and someone. It must have been in '38 or '39 when this occurred.

I remember every fall or every winter, Dad raised a bunch of hogs to kill, and we'd eat pork in the winter. The first thing I remember about killing hogs, Dad always shot them with a .22 when he got ready to kill them. I must have been four or five years old when I thought I was brave enough to go out and stand there and watch him kill the hog. Well, when he drew the bead of the gun and got right down over the hog and was fixing to shoot it, I couldn't stand it. I turned my head and couldn't watch.

Hog killing was an all-day operation. In fact, it might be two or three days if he could catch a good spell of winter. The way he would do it, he would take a 55-gallon barrel and dig a hole in the ground and set this barrel at about a 45-degree angle. They put water in the old wash pot and built a big fire around the wash pot to boil the water. After they got this water hot and everything was ready, they poured it in this barrel, and then he could go to the lot and kill the hog. I remember sometimes the hogs were extra-large, and he would take a horse or a team of horses and drag these hogs from the lot over to where they had the hot water. They would pick them up with hay hooks through their feet and throw them back and forth in this barrel of hot water. Then they would drag them out on a wooden platform, scrape them to get all the hair off, dress them, quarter them and hang the meat in the smokehouse after he had rubbed sugar cure on it.

I remember having to turn the sausage grinder, which was not very big, but it seemed it was awful hard for me to turn. I know that out in the smokehouse Dad would have a pile of meat cut up in chunks the size of a fist or smaller that was sausage meat, and this old hand grinder just clamped on the table. We'd turn this hand grinder and feed this meat through this hand grinder and, of course, he would usually season it before he ground it. And when he ground it, it would usually be put in cloth bags and hung up in the smokehouse. I remember him taking the hams and shoulders and doing what he called sugar curing them. He would buy prepared sugar cure, I believe it was Martin Sugar Cure, and he would rub these hams and shoulders several times for several different days to draw the water out and cure the hams. That was the only meat we had most of the time.

I remember moving from Roscoe to Blackwell, and we started probably a week or so before we really moved the furniture and the family down there. Moving the farm with all the plows, cultivators, horses, mules, even the feed we had left and so forth, required several trips as all that had to be moved. They moved it all in a wagon. I remember one load Dad had this old 1926 model Dodge, and we pulled a trailer behind it. I was riding with him. Between Blackwell and Sweetwater there is what they called "nine-mile hill." We were going down this hill and to me—from around Roscoe where I was raised in the flat country—that hill looked like an awfully steep hill and off to the side of the road it went almost straight down. I remember asking Dad what would happen if we ran off the side of that road and went off down that hill. I remember just as plain as day, he said, "Well, Son, I imagine we will scatter our tools."

I remember up at Busby, evidently in 1936 or '37, seemed like it was a pretty dry year, and there was a shortage of feed. Anyway, there was a feed store or something in Sweetwater that would buy mesquite beans. I remember that Ray and I would pick those things up, and we would get ten cents a bushel for them. Seemed like we picked two, three or four dozen bushels of mesquite beans, put them in a basket and carried them to town and sold them.

In the summer time we used to get our baths in the water trough, either that or in the tank. We had a pretty good size tank there in the pasture. If it would rain enough to keep water in the tank, we'd go down there and go swimming and take our bath at the same time. If the tank was low, we had a tin water trough, which was filled from the windmill. The windmill ran water in this tin trough all the time, and we would go out there and take a bath. In the winter time, we'd heat water and take a bath in a No. 3 wash tub in the kitchen. Carl Preston, Ray and myself would all take a bath in the same water, one at a time. I had to bathe in water after Carl Preston and Ray. I am not sure, but I think *[we took baths]* about once a week.

Mother always had chickens, and she sold eggs to help make a living. I remember in the spring when she would be raising little chickens, if there came up a cloud, we'd all have to get out there and chase the chickens into the chicken house. A lot of times they would scatter, and it would be awfully hard to get them all in before the cloud hit. In fact, I remember sometimes the cloud hitting with the wind blowing pretty hard, and we were still out trying to get the chickens in the chicken house.

She also sold butter and cream when we lived up at Busby. Ray and I did the milking. We would feed the cows cottonseed and milk them while they ate. We had fun squirting each other with milk. We could aim the cow's tit at each other and squeeze it to squirt each other. We would milk eight or ten cows, and Mother would either just sell cream or churn the butter. Mother would put the milk in one-gallon buckets and the cream would rise to the top. She would skim the cream off and churn it into butter. She had a one-pound butter mold to press this butter into a square pound of butter that she would sell, or Dad would take it to town and sell or trade for groceries. Later we had an old hand-turned cream separator. We would milk the cows, then run this milk through the cream separator and separate the skim milk from the cream.

I remember one sad thing about this. Our dining table had one big leg in the middle with arms sticking out from it to steady it. Mother had several gallons of milk on it that she was skimming the cream off of it to make butter. She had all the milk on one end of the table and the table turned over and spilled all of the milk. Ray and I were upstairs and heard the noise, and we ran downstairs, and mother was crying. I felt so sorry for her. It was grocery money she lost. I helped her clean it up. The milk buckets I spoke of before were syrup buckets that dad bought cane syrup in. Cane syrup and butter was dessert to us on biscuits. We would probably eat a gallon a month

The first lights or anything resembling electricity we had was evidently in about 1936 or '37 when Dad bought a wind-charger. That was nothing more than a generator with a wind propeller mounted on it that fit on top of the house. It looked like a miniature windmill, sort of, and this thing would charge batteries that you had in the house. It was more or less like a battery in a car. In fact, that is what the charger used, about four car batteries. That furnished our lights and our radio. Along about that time I remember our first radio. We had a little Zenith table model radio, and I remember very well listening to "The Lone Ranger" in the afternoon and "Lum and Abner," and "Amos 'n' Andy," the three programs I remember hearing when I was a kid.

It was on this same radio that we heard about Pearl Harbor. We still had it at that time, and I remember all of us gathering around it that Sunday afternoon, December 7, 1941, and listening to the news as it came over the radio about what had happened at Pearl Harbor. I believe I am right, seems like the next day after that they had recordings of the actual attack. Seems like you could hear those Jap planes coming over and hear the bombs exploding. I could be mistaken about this, but I don't think so as it seems like I remember that we heard that on the radio.

The first car I remember after I got big enough to pay attention to cars was a 1933 Ford that Dad bought used. What I mean is that this is the first car that I was old enough to really pay attention to and enjoy. I remember several older cars, the '23 and '26 model Dodge, and seemed like we had a Model A Ford or two in between that, but this was the first one that really registered on me after I was big enough to be proud of a car. The next car we had after this, in fact the car that I learned to drive in, was a 1939 Ford. It was the first car we had with hydraulic brakes, and the first car we had with a radio in it. We were proud of the one with a radio.

One other thing I remember going back a few years talking about the old cars, the old '23 and probably the '26 model Dodge had wooden spoke wheels. In dry weather, of course, that wood would dry and shrink somewhat and those old wheels would squeak. You would be driving down the road, and they would just squeak, squeak, squeak. I remember several times when before we'd start to town, we'd take and pour water on the wheels. It seems like one time, Dad just drove the old car out in the tank and let it set so the wood in the old wheels would swell up and they wouldn't squeak so when we were going down the road.

Sometime in the forties, Ray and I bought a 1928 Model A Ford coupe for $75. We bought it together, but shortly after that Ray went to Dallas to work, and I ended up with the old car. In fact, my senior year in high school, I drove that car from Busby to Sweetwater to high school, and I also used this old Model A going to work. The last half of my senior year I just had to go to school half a day so I drove that car to school. I got out at noon and played pool some afternoons. Then I got a job at the Gyp Mill and have been on my own ever since.

One more thing about the 1928 Model A. When it rained the roads got ruts eight to ten inches deep so you just drove slow in the ruts. One time Jack Whitworth (Joe's brother) needed to go to town, and his old car was out of order so I took him in my Ford. There was one place about a hundred yards long that had deep ruts so instead of going in the ruts at a slow speed. I put the Model A in second gear and split the ruts going about twenty-five or thirty miles per hour. I remember Jack holding on to the dash. He said when we got back that if he ever had to go to town with me in the rain *[again]* that he would damn sure *have* to go. Jack is the man I hoed cotton for at one dollar a day.

One time Dad made a good deal for me. He had equipment to sell and took in a saddlehorse named "Charlie" in trade. Ray had already moved to Dallas so I had Charlie to myself. There was four or five boys around Busby that had horses, and we had a lot of fun riding around Busby. Dad bought me a new saddle at Sears for twenty dollars. Me and the others built us a roping pen in our pasture. We bought us four goats to rope. I think we paid two dollars each. After we roped them a few times, they would run over to the fence, stop and stick their head against the fence so we couldn't rope them. We finally butchered one goat and cooked him out in the pasture. The boys I roped with and had other fun with were J.R. Graves, Milton Schweter, and J.H. and Morris Guelker.

None of the farmhouses that I remember living in had a bathroom. Of course, I mentioned before how we all took our baths, and we had an outdoor toilet for other purposes.

I remember when I wasn't too awfully old, I never had drank a Coke. I don't know why I associated Coke with chocolate, but I thought a Coke was chocolate. I don't remember where we were going, but we were in Sweetwater seems like, and we stopped at this service station, and Dad said we could have a Coke. I remember that that was the biggest disappointment there was to me because I didn't like it at all. It was too strong for me and, of course, I was expecting *chocolate milk* instead.

One time Ray and I got on Mother's nerves, and she finally lost her patience and grabbed something and started hitting us with it. When she finally looked to see what it was—Ray and I had already noticed because it didn't hurt a bit—it was just an old bonnet slat which is just about an inch-wide strip of cardboard cut-out of a shoebox. When she saw what she was whipping us with, she got tickled. In fact, we all got tickled about it.

I remember my mother as a kind, understanding, affectionate person. Also, she was intelligent. When there was an argument involved and she was in it, she was usually right.

My older brother Carl Preston Lewis, who died in 1937 as a result of a football injury—at the time I was eleven years old—was sixteen at that time. I remember him as an adult. It seems like my earliest recollection of him was as an adult or grown man. Of course, I realize now that he wasn't, but that is the way I picture him and the way I remember him. Carl was playing football with Roby High School in 1937. In a game at Colorado City, he tackled a boy and it swung him around and his leg hit another boy and broke the small bone in his leg. After his death Mother and Dad said that Ray and I could not play football.

I don't remember doing much with Carl Preston as he was five years older than me. He played the French harp very good. I remember him playing *Under the Double Eagle* on the harmonica. That was pretty. The sad thing that I remember was the night he died. Ray and I were upstairs in bed sometime around midnight. Dad and Marie came home and told Mother and the other girls that Carl had died, and we heard Mother and the other sisters crying and screaming. It was so sad.

I guess all of us kids had to work pretty hard, raised up on the farm. In planting the cotton crop, the first thing you do is plant it, of course, a seed every three or four inches apart. We planted cotton in April and May. After it came up, we had to chop it, which meant we had to take a hoe and thin it. If it was planted and it all came up, it would be too thick so we had to thin it out, try to leave a stalk about every ten or twelve inches. After the cotton got up and began to make, it had to be picked or pulled. It was all picked by hand. Way back in my early years, we didn't do anything but pick cotton, which was pull the cotton out of the burr and leave the burr on the stalk. In later years when the gins got to where they could handle it, we pulled it burr and all, put it in the trailer and carried it to the gin that way. We started picking or pulling cotton around the last of September and didn't finish sometimes until January. Dad nailed two-by-six lumber on the backside of the wagon where he hung the scales. We would weigh the sack and then dump it in the wagon. When the wagon was full, he would pull it to the gin with the horses. I remember getting to go to the gin with him one time. We sat on the top of the load of cotton to drive the horses. It was on the Forrester place where I was born so I had to be only four or five years old. We tried to finish picking cotton by Christmas, but some time we did not make it. I remember my first cotton sack. It was a tow sack that mother put a strap on it to go around my shoulder. I was so proud of it.

There was no such thing as a rotary hoe back then. Dad used a two-by-twelve piece of lumber and drove big nails in it to make a scratcher. I can remember riding an old mule and pulling a two-row scratcher at Busby.

One job I hated was cleaning out the henhouse. It had lumber boards that the hens roosted on. They were about four feet above the floor. About once a month Ray and I had to clean the droppings from under the roost. It was a very dirty and stinky job, but I was glad to do it for my mother and help her sell eggs to buy us groceries.

Mother kept a five-gallon bucket in the kitchen to put all the table scraps in to feed to the hogs. It was called a slop bucket. Ray or I had to carry it to the pen to feed the hogs.

I had to help my older sisters wash clothes outside. The first washing machine or anything resembling a washing machine was nothing but just an old hand wringer. It was just a stand that you put a tub on either side of it, and it had two rubber rollers and a handle sort of like a hand-crank ice cream freezer. You turned the handle, and one person would get on one side of it and another on the other side, usually Mother and one of the girls, and they would wash clothes in hot water, and one of the kids would stand there and turn this wringer and feed the clothes through, and they would fall out of the wringer into another tub with the rinse water on the other side. She used this thing up until about 1935 or '36, and then I remember that they got a Maytag washing machine, which was a little gasoline motor-driven washing machine that was somewhat easier to use and wasn't nearly so much work to it. The water, though, still had to be heated in a wash pot outside over a wood fire.

Some of Dad's work horses were mares. All the male horses were castrated. When the mares came in heat, I had to ride them about five miles to Claytonville, where a man kept a stud horse and a male donkey. If Dad wanted mules, the mare was bred to a jack donkey. If he wanted a horse colt, the mare was bred to a stud horse.

Dad always raised maize to feed the horses that he worked, and the way we gathered it was just to head it. We'd take a knife and a sled and go to the field with a horse hooked to this sled. The old horses were trained where you could tell them to "get up" and they would walk up two or three steps while you headed up three or four feet and threw the maize in this box. When you got up to this box, you would tell the horse to "get up" a little bit further and head on up to it. That is the way the maize was gathered.

Talk about heading maize, one time I was driving one sled and Ray was driving the other, and it seemed like we had, I suppose, Myrt and Marie, one in my sled and one in Ray's sled. We started home at noon or at night, I forget which, and we decided we'd have a little race. Ray and I got these old horses trotting and, like I say, each one of us in a sled with one of the sisters with us. We came around the corner behind the barn, and Dad had dug out some holes there to back the trailer into to load a cow or something. I'm not sure whether it was mine or Ray's sled, but a runner on one of these sled hits a hole and turned over. Of course, for a few minutes we weren't very popular with our sisters over that.

We always had a watermelon and a cantaloupe patch, too. I didn't like the watermelons when they were hot. In fact, the only time I that I really enjoyed a watermelon when I was a kid was when we'd go to the patch pretty early before they had a chance to get hot and they were still cool. That's the way I enjoyed eating a watermelon.

Maybe I shouldn't tell this, but some of the little meaner tricks Ray and I used to do is we had one old mule we headed maize with or hooked to a wagon hauling in maize. For some reason or other, every time you would punch this old mule, she'd break wind. Ray and I were just big enough to think that this was really funny.

I also spoke of the outdoor toilet earlier. Something else that Ray and I used to do that I guess you might say was a little bit mischievous was we'd delight in catching some of the girls in the toilet. We'd get out there fairly close and hit it with rocks. They, of course, didn't go for that very well either.

Of course I can't make this tape without telling this story. It has been told several times on Ella Mae or Eller, as we called her when we were kids and now. But anyway, along back I guess I was probably eight or nine, Ray eleven or twelve and Eller about thirteen. Ray and I decided to build us a trolley, which was a cable tied up in the top of a tree, and you slipped a piece of round pipe about two feet long over this cable, and you anchored this cable to another tree off about forty or fifty yards, though I don't remember just how far it was. Anyway, you would pull this pipe up into this tree and get ahold of the pipe and then just turn loose and ride down this cable. Well, back then, we didn't have any good strong cable to use so we gathered up all the old wire we could find and made us a makeshift cable, and we were a little bit afraid to try it ourselves. So, we hit on the bright idea of talking Eller into climbing up in this tree and riding this trolley down under the pretense that we were just going to let her be first. What we really wanted to know was if the wire was strong enough to hold *us*. And of course, Eller got up in there and started out, and she got about four feet down out of the tree, and the wire broke. She fell flat on her back eight, ten or twelve feet out of this tree. It scared her and scared us a little, too, I guess. It knocked the breath out of her, and she started yelling that she was going to the house and tell Mom and Dad on us. It seemed like the best I remember Ray and I held her out behind the barn. I don't know what we offered, but we talked her out of it. I remember that she was crying, "I can't talk. I can't talk" because it knocked the breath out of her. Anyway, we finally got her breathing back and made a few promises and talked her out of going to tell on us, got her in a good humor, and that was the way it all wound up.

Eller also accuses us of finding her paper dolls that she had cut out and kept in a shoe box under the bed. I don't remember this, and I don't think Ray or I either one would do such a thing. She says one time she remembers going to get her paper dolls and found a bunch with their heads torn off. Like I say, this is sort of an unexplainable situation, and I don't know exactly who is right about it.

Something else that comes to mind that Ray and I did, which I guess was a little bit on the mischievous side, is evidently when Juanita was about six or seven years old, which would make me eight or nine, something along in there, Mother and Dad bought her a tricycle for Christmas. They got it a few weeks ahead of Christmas and hid it out in the barn in the cottonseed. Ray and I sort of stumbled on to it one day the best I remember, and we would slip out there in the barn before Christmas and get this tricycle out and ride it. Of course, the only place we had to ride it was in the cow lot, and I'm sure probably one of us watched while the other one rode it. In fact, we would get it out there in the soft cow pile and spin the wheels. I don't remember just exactly whether we were caught at it or Juanita ever knew it or not, but I know we would carry buckets of water out there and washed that tricycle half a dozen times before Christmas.

Sort of recapping all of my school career, I started school at Brownlee and went the first half of my first year at Brownlee, then we moved to Blackwell. I went through the second half of my first year, second grade and the first half of my third year at Blackwell. Then we moved to Busby, and I finished up the third grade and on through grammar school at Busby. About the time I was ready to go into high school at Busby, they closed the school so we rode the bus to Sweetwater. I went the last three years of high school in Sweetwater and graduated there in 1943. That was a sad [school] year for us because that was the year we lost Mother. In fact, she passed away the first day of my senior year.

I finished up that school year. Then immediately after I got out of high school, I went to work for the gyp mill there in Sweetwater. It was the U.S. Gypsum Company, and I remember I was working from three in the afternoon until midnight at sixty cents per hour. I have been on my own ever since. Seems like it was about six months that I worked there at the gyp mill during the war, and they [government] wouldn't allow you to change jobs. You were what they called frozen to a job. You couldn't quit. I'm not sure just what all the details were, but you had to have a very good reason to quit a job and move to another one.

Anyway, I had this chance to go to work for International Harvester Company, which I really wanted to do, so I went ahead and quit the gyp mill in spite of the waiting period. You could go ahead and quit, but when you quit one job you had to wait six weeks before you could take another job. Of course, help was in demand because a lot of people couldn't get help. During these six weeks, there was a Texaco service station in Sweetwater that hired me. I forgot this old man's name in that station, but he said that he didn't care whether I was froze on one job or not. He needed some help, and he would hire me. I worked for him that six weeks before I went to work for International Harvester.

I worked for International Harvester for about two years, then I went into the Merchant Marines for two and a half years. When I got out of the Merchant Marines, I went back to work for International Harvester and worked until 1949 in Sweetwater. Then they transferred me over to Abilene. That was a lucky move because that is where I met Jurdene Gentry and in a short time married her.

There are a few more things that come to mind that we used to do when we were kids as a pastime. One of them was when it would rain, we would get out in the road. Of course, these were just dirt roads up to the house, and these roads were packed real hard. When it rained they would get slick. I remember going out there barefooted and making what we called a skating rink, which was nothing more than just getting out there barefooted and running and sliding on the hard dirt. We could slide ten or twelve feet. I don't remember looking to see if there were any nails or glass or anything in the dirt. I don't know how we kept from ruining our feet, but I don't remember any of us ever getting hurt doing it.

We also used to take old tires and curl up inside them. One of us would push the other one, just roll him down the road in this old tire, and him just going around curled up inside the tire. We also used to take a couple of old cultivator wheels and just put a round shaft or an axle between them and spread them out about four or five feet apart. When we were at Blackwell, we would get up on those hills and just sit on this bar. It wasn't anything in the world but just two wheels and an axle between them. We would sit on this bar and ride that thing off these hills. You had no control or no steering whatsoever. I don't ever remember getting hurt on the thing. I don't know how we kept from it because if you saw you were going to hit a tree or a rock or run off into the creek or something, your only means of escape was to bail off the back and let it go.

Rubber guns also were a big when we were kids. We would make them out of wood and put a clothespin on the back of the pistol grip. On the back of the pistol grip, you snagged a rubber band that you cut out of an old tire inner tube on this clothespin. Then you stretched it over the end of this barrel. Then when you gripped the pistol, you released the clothespin and fired the rubber band, which would shoot several feet. Used to Ray and I and some of our Lewis cousins when they would come up would choose sides and have great wars with these rubber guns. Another way we used to make them would be more or less a rifle type of gun. We would take a longer piece of wood and back about where the action would be on a gun we would cut a bunch of notches an inch apart. We would take a fishing cord or a string right in front of these notches and we would lay this string down across these notches and then put a rubber band in each notch. A lot of times we would have six or eight notches, and we would load six or eight rubber bands, one in each notch. Then when you pulled this string from the back, it would release one rubber band at a time or if you pulled the string pretty fast in rapid fire action it would shoot six or eight rubbers or however many you had on the gun. We called it a machine gun.

Along this same line I also remember we used to have corncob fights. Mother and Dad, of course, would put up corn when they canned corn in the fall. Whenever we cooked this corn, she would cut it off the cob and just can the kernels. Of course all these cobs would just be thrown behind the barn. We would get out there and pick up a bunch of those cobs, and one get on one side of the barn and one on the other, and we would throw those wet cobs at each other. Those things got pretty heavy and soggy, and it hurt pretty good when you got hit up the side of the head with one of them.

The first vacation or anything I remember resembling a vacation other than just an occasional fishing trip was going back to Blackwell to Myrt's and Bill's. They got married, and we moved to Busby, and there was a period there of probably three or four or five years when Ray and I would get to go down there together and spend one or two weeks with Myrt and Bill. This was in the summer time, of course, after we had sort of caught up with our cotton chopping. That used to be one of the very highlights of our summer, getting to go down there and spend that time at Myrt and Bill's. Also along the latter part of this same time, I remember spending quite a bit of time with Mildred and Arnold. They lived out east of town there. This place that they lived on had a cliff or a mountain off down in the pasture and for some reasons the buzzards flew around this. We used to go down there and take our slingshots. As those buzzards would sail around those cliffs, we would take our slingshots and shoot at them.

Speaking of Myrt, I also remember that before she and Bill got married, she went and bought some baby chickens. She was going to raise these chickens so they would have some chickens to start off with when they got married. I don't even remember how many she had or anything, but one night before they got married a skunk got in there and killed a bunch of her chickens. I know she was pretty well upset, and we all felt sorry for her over the situation.

As I said before, I was with International Harvester and was transferred to Abilene in 1949. That's where I met Jurdene. We got married September 4, 1949, and lived in Abilene until 1953, then moved to Midland. I had always thought to myself and, after we got married, told Jurdene that I would like to have two boys, and I feel very fortunate that that is the way things turned out.

John Preston was born in May of 1950, and Jurdon Marc was born in January of 1954. I remember very well the morning Preston was born. I was, of course, excited I know. In fact, I couldn't get Jurdene and Mrs. Gentry ready to go to the hospital as fast as I thought we ought to get there. When Preston was born, and they brought him out of the delivery room, I was standing there and the nurse had him in this blanket and pulled this blanket back where I could see him. I was quite shocked because I thought he looked just like me. In fact, I told Mrs. Gentry that he looked just like me.

I remember when Preston was just a baby, he was probably eight or nine months old, I had to go to Dallas to a school down there. It was the first time I had ever been away from him after he was born and, as far as I remember, even away from Jurdene after we got married. I remember getting on the train there in Abilene that afternoon, and Preston just threw a fit. He cried and wanted to go with his daddy. It was pretty hard for me to leave. In fact, I had to stay down there about a week, and that was the first commercial airplane ride I ever took as I was in such a hurry to get back home that I flew from Dallas back to Abilene instead of riding the train.

Of course when Marc was that age, he would cry to go with anyone, Joe and Ella Mae, mostly, but he had going on his mind, and whoever was leaving, he wanted to go with them. It didn't make any difference.

I will try to add a few humorous things that happened to the boys as they were growing up. One time when Preston was about two years old, he had had some sort of sickness. We had had the doctor out to give Preston a shot. Of course, that was the first experience Preston had had with a doctor or a shot that he could remember. Along a few days after that, I was walking down the hall, and Preston was walking in behind me and he kept saying "Daddy, Daddy," and finally I stopped. When I did, he stuck me in the seat with a pin. I turned around and said, "Why son, what are you doing?" and he said, "Daddy, I's just giving you a shot."

When we lived in Abilene, and Preston was still somewhere around two years old, two and a half probably, Jurdene let him play out in the yard with the water hose. She looked out there one day, and he had this water hose. He had on a little pair of training pants, and he had that hose stuck down his training pants cooling off.

Also, this same time there was one of the neighbor's dogs that came over and started up in the front yard. Preston saw this dog, and he took off after him with this water hose and squirted him until the dog ran down the street. Preston got real tickled. He thought he had really done something.

Also, Jurdene was in town one time, and she was in a service station to get some gas. They pulled up to the gas pumps and Preston said, "Mother, I know that there is three kinds of gas." And she said, "What's that?" He replied, "Ethyl, regular and filler-up."

Preston was always real good to look after Marc when Marc was a baby. And one time they were out in the yard, and we heard Preston just screaming at the top of his voice. We went around there, and Marc was just about to pick up a tarantula. He had screamed for us before Marc picked up the tarantula.

One time when Marc was about three years old, his grandfather and grandmother Gentry came out to see us. They went down to the chicken house, grandmother and Marc did, and walked into the chicken pen. Grandmother said Marc looked up at her and said, "Grandmother, do you smell that?" She said, "Well, yes, I do." He said, "It sure does smell big, dudn't it?"

Along about 1958 I believe it was, I bought the boys a donkey for them to learn to ride on. We bought him out south of Sweetwater on the Double Heart Ranch and rented a U-Haul trailer to haul him back to Midland. Of course, the boys were certainly proud of this donkey. I suppose at that time they didn't know too much difference between a donkey and a horse. Anyway, they were real proud of it and named him "Flash." And we rented this U-Haul trailer and were bringing him back to Midland. We came through Big Spring, I believe it was, that Sunday afternoon. There were some kids on the street and one of them saw us coming down the street, and he brayed like a donkey with his hands up above his head like a pair of donkey ears. They were laughing, and it sort of insulted Marc and Preston. They couldn't figure out why those boys were laughing at their donkey.

After we had this old donkey awhile, I walked out by the back and saw Marc in the pen. He had a little old bow and arrow that we'd bought him. The arrows had a rubber suction cup on the end. He was stalking this donkey from behind, and he slipped up to within about four feet of this donkey and drew back the bow and arrow and shot the old donkey right in the hind end. In the meantime, I had sort of slipped out there pretty close to the lot fence. When he hit this old donkey, I heard him say, "Bull's eye."

I have said we had to make our own toys as kids. Back then if we had anything to play with, we had to make it. I guess that is one reason I wanted Preston and Marc to have old Flash and a porter-car *[go-cart]* I built them.

Along about the time Marc was between two and three years old and Preston would have been between six and seven, we were driving around one Sunday afternoon, and we drove by the hospital where Marc was born. Preston said, "Mother is that where we got Marc?" And she said, "Yes." Preston said—of course this was before they even knew anything about the birds and the bees—"Well, Mother, did you just lay an egg?" And Marc, he put his hand on his hips and said, "Preston, you know my mother is not a chicken."

This is July 1974 and the boys are both grown now and married. Both have given us daughters-in-law we are very proud of. Jurdene and I wish you all health, happiness and prosperity through life.

John Bracken Lewis
Midland, Texas
1974

CHAPTER NINE

Juanita Myrle Lewis Roberts

When I try to think back to my childhood days, it's difficult for me to decide when I really began to remember what was happening, so maybe some of the things will be from having heard them told a time or two.

I was born near Roscoe, Texas, December 11, 1928, on what I believe was the Forrester place. I was the last of eight children, so I am sure I got by with a lot of things the others didn't. I know they had to work harder than I did in the fields, but I love my family and feel privileged to have been born into a very loving family.

I do not remember very much about living at Blackwell. One thing I think I remember is the hand swing over the creek. I begged Ella Mae to let me swing, and when she finally gave in she didn't push me quite hard enough to come back to her, and she finally talked me into dropping off. I fell into a tub Dad had in the creek to water the cows in. It really wasn't a very comfortable landing.

I must have been about five years old when we moved to the Busby community north of Sweetwater. We had an upstairs that we kids slept in. I remember a few times slipping up the stairs just part way and listening to Ella Mae and her girlfriends' conversation. I don't remember just what all was said, but it was fun to eavesdrop.

In our backyard we had three trees grouped together. I made a playhouse among those trees and spent many hours there with the cat and dogs as my playmates. That is as long as they would put up with me. I used jar lids for plates, little jars for glasses and sticks for silverware, or whatever I could find to use. I made very good mud pies in my playhouse.

We had two dogs named "Nip" and "Tuck." In the early spring or fall the dogs and I would curl up on the front porch and take a nap, but those two dogs would get mad at one another and have a dogfight deluxe. They would chew each other up pretty bad. Dad would doctor them to get the places to heal without infection. We also had a mulberry tree in the front yard with lots of mulberries on it. We have had several mulberry fights. I think I may have been an onlooker more than taking a part in it, but I do remember when you got hit with one you knew you had been hit. It would sting very much and leave a nice red spot.

I remember one time Mother and Dad had gone to town, leaving we four younger ones at home. J.B. got mad at Ray about something and was chasing him around the cistern. He had, I think, a pair of scissors in his hands, and Ray was laughing at him. Ella Mae was crying and chasing them with a broom trying to stop them. She was scared to death as to what might happen. I don't remember how it stopped, whether they just ran down or Ella Mae got them to stop. It seemed like they waited until Mother and Dad left before they got crossways, and Ella Mae would try to make peace. Oh, but we had our good times, especially when we made chocolate fudge and one of the boys got the Watkins liniment instead of the vanilla. There was some real spitting and sputtering going on. This also happened when Mother and Dad went to town.

I remember one year not long after we moved to Busby, Dad and the boys went hunting. There was a big snow, and they came back with rabbits. We had fried rabbit for supper. They used to bring home squirrel, also. Mother would let us go out and get a bucket of snow to make some snow ice cream, which was very good.

I became rather excited about the time to head maize because Dad would allow me to go along. I would ride on the sled, that is until one time I grabbed a head of maize and cut my finger pretty bad, so that ended that. I still carry the scar on my finger.

We had a smokehouse that Dad put his sugar-cured meats in. It smelled so good, but then one year Dad hired two husbands and their wives to pull bolls. If I remember right, they didn't stay but a week or two. Dad cleaned out the smokehouse for them to stay in. When they got paid on the weekend, the two men got into town someway and didn't come home for a night or two, then they were drunk, so dad fired them. While the men were gone, the two women walked down the road about three-quarter mile to a vacant house and climbed the windmill tower, staying two or three hours, finally climbed down and came back to the house. I remember being at the wagon when the two women brought their sacks of cotton to empty them. One climbed over into the wagon and tore her pants, she thought. When the other asked if she tore them, she said, "No, I didn't tear them, but I sure did scratch them good."

I think I used to make my sisters a bit unhappy at me. You see when it came time to wash the dishes I always seemed to develop a terrific need to go to the toilet. Somehow my needs were such that the dishes would be finished before I got back to the house. I always thought that rather neat timing!

I also remember the "uptown toilet" that Dad built at Busby. It had a cement floor with a seat shaped like a commode, also of cement. A little warmer in winter than the past ones had been. At least the wind did not blow in on you, as the bottom section was closed in, and we were happy about that.

As the time came for me to start to school, I sure did dread it. One day, for some reason, I had to walk to school by myself, and it was so foggy you could hardly see anything, but Dad instructed me to follow the fence line and said I could not miss the school. Of course, I cried and didn't want to go, but I did. And sure enough, I made it just fine.

Dad was on the school board for a year or two, and sometimes J.B., Mother and I would go to Busby to Cumbie's store. Mother would visit with Mrs. Cumbie while Dad was in the school board meeting. There were times when Dad gave J.B. and me some money to spend. I had maybe a nickel or so more than J.B., but he convinced me that because he had more pieces, he had more money and got me to trade with him. I don't remember if he told me the difference after trading, or if Mother and Dad told me. Anyway, Dad got on to him pretty good. He seemed to have had more candy than I so naturally I was somewhat disappointed.

There was one particular time that J.B. and I were in the car alone. I do not remember if we were home or somewhere waiting on Mother and Dad, but anyway J.B. pushed the cigarette lighter in, leaving it just long enough to make it good and hot, but not red. He asked me to touch it and see if it was hot, so in trying to please my brother, I touched and it was definitely hot. Needless to say, I had the print of the lighter on my index finger for some time afterwards.

Santa Claus bought me a tricycle for Christmas after we moved to Busby, and I was so happy with it. But it was a somewhat "short-lived" tricycle. You see my brothers Ray and J.B. got on it one day with J.B. on the seat, Ray on the back with his hands also on the handlebars leaning his weight over them to ride down the hill to the mailbox. Well, they didn't make it as their weight bent the front wheel all out of shape, to a point that it could not be repaired. Ray has since confessed to the fact that he and J.B. would slip it out of the cottonseed bin before Christmas, where Dad thought he had it hid and ride it in the cow lot through all the cow piles, spinning the wheels and having a ball with it. They would take it to the cow trough and wash all the "cow stuff" off and put it back in the cottonseed bin. So I guess I was lucky to have even gotten it in one piece. Dad had told them to be sure I did not come out there and find it so I guess they were "guarding" it!

Something else I used to have fun doing was playing in the cottonseed bin, piling cottonseed up higher and jumping off into it. I had to entertain myself, since we had no close neighbors to come to play or to go visit. However, as I grew older, I used to walk about one-and-a-half to two miles up the road to the Casey place. They had a daughter named Pauline who was about my age. We rode horses and a number of things that I did not get to do any other place. Pauline was an only child, and they were more financially able to get her things than Dad with his large family, but to me I was more fortunate than her because of my loving family and the fun and enjoyment we had just being together.

I don't know if J.B. remembers this or not but I can see it now. He again was chasing Ray through the barn. This time as they came dashing through the door, J.B. stepped on a piece of baling wire which went through his foot to the very outer layer of skin. I doubt he remembers, but I cried about as much as he did. Dad pulled it out, I think. Anyway, he had to soak it in kerosene for some time. He got out of chores for a few days.

I'm sure I will be repeating several things others have written, like when J.B. and Ray talked Ella Mae into trying their trolley in the tree behind the barn. Of course it broke, leaving her bottom imprint in the dirt very clearly, knocking the breath from her, scaring all of us to pieces. Pete held Tis behind the barn with Jaber's help, except when he held me so I could not go to the house to tell Mother. Ella Mae, when she could manage to get enough breath, would beg me to run to get Mother.

I used to entertain myself a lot by going swimming in the metal tank that Dad had at the barn for the cows to drink from. It was quite refreshing on hot days. One day I was swimming and a car drove up with two men in it. Mother and Dad were gone and I was scared to death because I was afraid they were coming to the barn, but they walked about the yard a minute or two, then left. I did not know who they were, and they never knew I was in the tank, thank goodness, but I stayed as low down in the water as possible.

Dad raised several hogs for meat. It was always exciting at hog-killing time as we had a lot of good meat to eat. Of course, I always enjoyed eating. I remember Mother canning sausage in the big-size cans. Mother kept milk in gallon buckets on the porch to sour, then scraping the cream off to churn for butter. That was part of my job to churn the butter. I did not really like to churn, but sure enjoyed the butter. I also used to go out and ride the big hogs for a horse. It was fun until they dumped you in their mud puddle, but that did not happen but once because I learned quickly to jump off when they headed in that direction. Of course, most of these tricks I learned from my brothers.

In the winter time our bathtub was a No. 3 tub sitting behind the coal heating stove in the kitchen. That was the only room heated in the winter. It wasn't so bad when you were first to bathe, but sometimes there was little more hot water added for the next one to bathe in. But I don't believe we are none the worse because of it.

One thing I remember was how excited I would be to get to go to see the girls at Blackwell. I do not remember how old J.B. and I were, but Bill was going to teach us how to "Indian wrestle." I don't believe Bill and Myrt had been married too long, but anyway Indian wrestling was done by intertwining one's legs every way possible. But I guess Bill was too successful because one time of the leg twisting I broke wind and that put an end to the Indian wrestling. Oh, how embarrassed I was! We also enjoyed tramping over the creek bed, going wading in the water and climbing on the hills about, carving our initials on the big rocks on the big bluffs on the side of the hill.

One time at Busby, Carl Preston had an old car of some kind that Dad had been able to get for him to drive to Roby school so he could stay for football practice. Anyway, one day it was pouring down rain and Carl stopped by Busby school to pick me up. Best I remember it didn't have any doors, so I had to ride over close to him so I would not fall out. He told me to hold onto his leg. When we got home, he told Mother I almost squished his leg off. I do not remember a lot about Carl Preston as I was only eight when we lost him, but it seemed to me that he had such a sweet disposition. He enjoyed so much for me to comb his hair while he sat in a rocking chair playing his harmonica until he would go sleepy. Next thing I knew, he would be asleep. I truly missed him.

As I grew older, I really enjoyed the various sports that we played in school. We would get so excited when another school would come to play ball, especially when we were not expecting them. I played guard on our basketball team. We played on dirt courts and I kept my knees skinned most all the time. We went to Capitola a few times to play when Ralph was teaching there, and he was always the referee. And, of course, I believed he picked on me, as it seemed every time I turned around he called a foul on me.

We also played a lot of baseball. I played third base most of the time. Once in awhile, I played first or shortstop. When they sent me to the junior high in Sweetwater, we had a rather long ride on the bus to school. Mr. Williams was our principal at junior high. He used to come out at noon and watch us play ball. When at bat, I could knock a home run with one hand. After that he called me "Lula-Bell." One day he walked into school with me after the lunch period, and I had for several years small warts on the back of my hand. They always became quite red when I played ball, and the period after lunch I got a note to come to the office. I was scared to death, but he only wanted to see my hand, as he thought I had measles or something. But when he found out what it was, he became rather tickled and wanted to know how I got them. I was relieved, yet a bit embarrassed. I also enjoyed playing tennis. I played in several tournaments in singles. I remember one time when I was in the ninth grade, the teacher in high school sent for me to play doubles in a tournament because she was short a player due to illness. I was always big for my age so I guess she thought I could pass for a high school student. I don't remember how far we got in the game, but it was fun while it lasted.

During the time Ralph was in the air force, we would get so excited when we heard an airplane that sounded rather low because it usually would be Ralph flying over to buzz the house. J.B. and I would run out into the field next to the house to throw dirt clods at him. He came close enough to see a big smile on his face. He would have a co-pilot, I guess, with him. One time Ralph's sister Arlene Ammons, Mary Francis Walker and myself rode the bus to San Angelo to a football game. We spent the weekend with Marie and Ralph as he was stationed there. They took us out to the airbase, and Ralph convinced us we had to salute the guards at the gate or else we would not be allowed to go in. Of course, he was watching in his rear-view mirror. We saluted all right, and I'm sure the guards thought we were nuts. They looked at us as if they thought we had a problem.

I guess I am jumping from later times back to earlier times, but I always looked forward to Joe coming to court Ella Mae. I always thought Joe was a No. 1 guy. I usually would be on the porch when he came, and he would sit down and talk to me awhile before going into the house. Also, he nearly always gave me some Dentyne chewing gum and that was a treat back then. I was polishing my shoes one time, and he gave me some good advice: "Always keep your shoes polished, and they would last longer" and I tried to do just that.

I shall never forget my first high-heel shoes. Dad took me to J.C. Penney. I must have been about thirteen; anyway, it was before we lost Mother. Mrs. Olsen was the lady Dad always had to wait on him. I had on white anklets, and Dad let me wear the high heels from the store. I was so proud of them, walking down the street feeling so dressed up with my anklets and high heels.

Dad somehow got Ella Mae a piano at Busby. She took a few lessons and could play some, but I enjoyed playing with it so much. I was able to pick out different songs I knew, and finally learned to chord with my left hand from Ella Mae. I also watched my third- and fourth-grade teacher, a Miss George, play the piano. She could really play one, too. I always wanted to play a piano, and the Lord just gave me the talent to play by ear. I used to sit at the window sill and pretend to play with the music on the radio, or just sing a song and play like I was playing the piano. I remember one time when Mildred and Arnold came to see us, I was playing a song that was a waltz, and Mildred and Arnold came in and danced to it. Arnold complimented me on my playing and that he enjoyed waltzing to it with Mildred. Miss George taught us music, and Dad bought me a harmonica to play. We made a lot of noise as we attempted to learn how to play the harmonicas.

I shall not forget when Dad bought a gasoline washing machine. It sure was loud, but it sure beat the rubboard. We had to heat water in the wash pot on an open fire in the yard. I usually helped the girls with washing when they came to stay with Mother after she got to a point of having to stay in bed. At least I thought I was helping. Sometimes I was not sure the girls were convinced of that, however.

After Joe and Ella Mae moved to Coleman where Joe worked for the railroad, I went home with them and spent a week. They lived in an apartment in the Santa Fe bunkhouse, and there were several families living there. Of course, there were several kids so we had a lot of fun playing various games. One girl I remember about my age named Betty Jean. We walked to town to go to a movie and window shop. We were doing good to have money for a movie, but we managed to do so occasionally.

After Mother's death, I had a rather difficult time to adjust to the changes that occurred. Dad remarried in a little over a year, and for a fourteen-year-old girl, it was not an easy event to accept. But of course, in later years I realized Dad being only forty-nine was too young to live the rest of his life alone. Finally, Dad and Beulah moved in close to Sweetwater, near the Freeman place where Joe and Ella Mae lived. For some reason I can't remember too much about this place. I don't think they stayed there too long until Dad bought the house on Ninth Street in Sweetwater. I believe Dad went to work for International Harvester when we first moved close to town.

It may be that Dad was living on the place just north of town when Mary Francis Walker and I went to Big Spring, Texas, to work at the State Mental Hospital. I watched over patients who were capable of working in the kitchen area. I had quite a number of new experiences there. They gave these people a dance one night a month, and that is where I met Hoyle Nix and his West Texas Cowboys Band. The girl he was dating at the time also worked in the office and was the switchboard operator at the hospital. So, that began my side job of playing the piano for Hoyle Nix and band. I must admit that would have been my life had it not been for the places we went to play music. But I love good music and enjoyed it for about six or eight months. The band came to Sweetwater to Dad's on Ninth Street one Sunday afternoon and played for them. I remember one night at a VFW Hall, we played for a dance, and I got thirteen dollars in tips, which was the most I ever got and was quite a bit to me.

I came back to Sweetwater for a short while and in 1944 I believe I went to live with Uncle Cliff and Aunt Gladys at Goose Creek, now known as Baytown. Let me digress a moment. Before going to Uncle Cliff's, I met and ran around with Mavoureen Clark in Sweetwater. She lived on Grape Street and her parents operated a washateria. It was through her that I met Walter Roberts, who was in the Army at the time. We corresponded during the time he was overseas and later married after he got out of the Army. Now on to Goose Creek and my going to high school for a year down there. Uncle Cliff and Aunt Gladys were real good to me. We used to go to Beaumont fairly often to see Uncle George and Aunt Sue. I enjoyed my time with them. I also worked at the Weingarten Grocery in the bakery. I remember one time a hurricane came inland that far and it was about 3:30 or 4 o'clock in the afternoon. It got so dark, as if it was midnight. The wind blew and rained as I have never seen it before. In the midst of all of this, I was to get off work, and I was really scared, but just before I was about to leave, in walked Uncle Cliff. I sure was glad to see him. He said he knew I would probably be scared and not know what to do, so he came after me. I told him he would never know how glad I was to see him walk through that door. Melba Hope, their daughter who was about five years old, and Aunt Gladys were in their car waiting. Uncle Arthur and Aunt Stella also lived there. Their son Wyatt and I used to go bowling quite a lot.

As I said before, I had met Walter Roberts through a girlfriend who was his cousin. When he returned from his overseas duties he was sent to Oklahoma to a hospital, as he had received an injury to his back. He was later sent to San Antonio to Fort Sam Houston to receive his discharge papers in January 1946. He came to Goose Creek to see me, and we made plans to be married on March 16, 1946.

The Lord has blessed us with three boys: Harvey, Gary and Wayland. They in turn have given us to this date eight grandchildren. Harvey with four, Tammy, Amy, Wendy and Corey; Gary with two Jamie Leiann and Jeffrey; and Wayland with two, Christopher and Chad. We are very thankful that the Lord has provided us with our family of sons, daughters-in-laws and grandchildren.

In drawing this to a close, I must say that I am most grateful to be a member of the N.P. Lewis family and will always cherish the love and joys along with the heartaches that we have all shared. My prayers for each one is that we will always honor God in our daily lives, and that His blessings shall be given unto each in obedience to His will.

Juanita Lewis Roberts,
Fort Worth, Texas
1985

CHAPTER TEN

Letters from the Farm

A mong my family possessions are a handful of letters sent between 1935 and 1941 by Ora Bell Garrett Lewis and three of her children to Mildred McRorey, their oldest sister who was nicknamed "DeDuse," a name variously misspelled by the kids in their letters as "DeDoes," "DeDoos," "DeDose," or "De-Doose." I have corrected those variations and other misspellings for the sake of readability. Likewise, I have corrected some grammar where it was needed for clarity, but not all mistakes. Ora Bell, for instance, often used a colon instead of a decimal in listing monetary amounts. I have left that variation intact. Where necessary, I included explanatory information bracketed in italics.

While the letters often talk about family and neighbors, they also give some insight into life during the Great Depression and the sense of community among kin and acquaintances. Though times were hard for nearly all Americans during this period, the Lewis family managed—sometimes better than their urban counterparts—because they were able to raise some of their own food and thus save their limited money for other needs.

These missives also offer a farm wife's perspective on the hard times like the hawks killing her chicks or making a payment on a gas-powered washing machine as well as the youthful observations of her children hoping to go to the circus or getting to visit Santa Claus at the Fisher County Courthouse.

From a personal standpoint, my favorite letter is from Ora on December 9, 1935, describing her children's activities at the moment, including the comment, "Well, I just don't know what Jaber is a doing. He has a pile of cotton here on the table that he took out of a stuffed dog." Jaber was the nickname for my father, who was a tinkerer all his life and was always taking things apart to see how they worked or what they were made of.

Perhaps the most insightful letters are dated September 30, 1935, and October 31, 1935. The first demonstrates the economics of the time after the sale of a single bale of cotton. The second from Ora and three of her children show how the family, including the young ones, contributed to their joint well-being by picking cotton, the primary source of their income.

Unlike their memoirs, these letter document life at the time rather than years later with the varnish of age softening the reality of the era.

Roby, Texas
Sept. 30, 1935
Dear Mildred,

Will write you tonight. Well the kids have just had a great argument how to spell pencil. J.B., Ray and Ella Mae, they have gotten quiet and decided that Papa and I maybe can spell it. Ella Mae was going to have her teacher write it down and show us it was spelled <u>pencle</u>.

Well we had lots of company this week. Cliff and Gladys came Wednesday about 2 o'clock and spent the night. Sat. morning Bill and Myrt, Cliff and Gladys came and ate dinner with us.

Marie, Goff and Jake came Sat. eve. After supper Andy, Clyde, Aunt Ione and Clint came after Jake.

Mrs. Hitt was operated on last week, had her womb taken out. Aunt Ione had a card Thursday, saying she was getting along alright. She thought she ought to have heard again Saturday but did not. After Jake came up here, they decided they would go down there so Jake didn't get to spend the night. Haven't heard no more from them. Goff is one more *[illegible]*, he is staying at Roy's and Bettie Mae's.

The hawks have begun to catch my little chicks. Papa, Bill and Cliff have all tried to shoot them, but they get away too fast.

The children stayed out of school Monday to pick cotton,

picked Monday morning and *[it]* went to raining so they couldn't go back to the field. They went to school Tue. and Wed., stayed out Thur., Fri. and finished the bale; picked part of it and pulled part of it; had on 1830 *[likely the weight in pounds of the haul]*, got a 518 *[-pound]* bale; sold it for 10:85 *[likely 10.85 cents per pound]*, got $6:23 out of seed after paying ginning. Made it bring him $62:56. We finished paying out the machine *[uncertain what this refers to]*, paid another payment on washing machine with $13 and some cents left.

Mildred, the pig man came. Papa and Marie picked four pigs, one male and three sows at $5 each, that left the man three. He told them they could have the other three for $12:50, and they jewed him down to $11:00. Marie gave a check for $21, and she gave one on you for $10. We are awful proud of them.

Edna Myrt was afraid you might think hard of her for coming off Sat. as you meant to come to her house. Bill said she didn't get that chance very often and thought you had just as soon come to her house next Saturday and stay over Sunday.

Gladys brought us another friendship pattern *[likely a quilting block]* to make one for Annie May. I'm like the little boy that was picking cotton. As fast as one sun went down they hung up another one (meaning the moon) so he had to pick all the time. (Don't get one block made till I have to make another) and as Juanita says (So there). Aunt Annie is in bad shape again (about five months) already going to Dr. with trouble she had before. They said they didn't know what outcome would be, were really uneasy about her.

I must write Aunt Bird tonight too so will close
With love
Mama
P.S. Went to see the Pittman girl a little while this afternoon. You know she was operated on last Tuesday a week ago. She seems to be doing fine. I took several magazines for her to read. She acted like she sure appreciated it.
So, Bye Bye
Mama
Tues. Morning
I have 100 cans of tomatoes now. Will gather a picking this morn

for relish. Glad your "Tom" turned out well. May have a few more if you want them. *Mama*

Sep 30, 1935
Monday Night
Dear DeDuse,

How are you this morning? I am all right. But I have just finished my arithmetic for tomorrow. Mr. Pritchard took up our history notebook, and he put on mine a very good A-. We are going to have a test tomorrow in History and the rest next few days. They are going to turn out Friday, if it don't rain.

I picked 47 pounds the first morning and it showered that evening; and we did not get to pick that evening. And I picked 69 the next day and I pulled 190, the next 30 the first weigh-in Saturday morning. Me and Jaber went in swimming Sunday evening. It was so cold we did not stay in very long. And while we were in, a duck or what we thought was a duck *[landed]* and *[we]* went to the house and told Bucky and he brought the gun down there and shot at it and crippled it so it could not fly or do nothing but swim around. When me and Jaber got in after it, every time we would get pretty close it would dart under the water and come up way in head of us. Finally Jabe caught it and it was a mud-hen.

Your Brother
Ray Lewis
Write soon

Sep 30, 1935
Dear DeDuse,

I think that I am going to make it all right in school. We are going to have a test tomorrow at school on arithmetic. We may go to the circus tomorrow. I hope we can go. Mama said we might go to school tomorrow and go to the circus tomorrow night. I hope we can go tomorrow night. I can see lots of animals that I never seen before. The little colt is growing. We have turned them in *[the]* stalk field. They are growing lots. Me and Ray saw a duck down on the tank. We went and got the shotgun and Bucky. Bucky shot the duck. He just crippled him. Me and Ray jumped into the tank When we would get *[with]*in about five feet of him he would go under the water, and we would see him come up a way out yonder. Finally, I caught him so we took him up to the house and he was a mud-hen so that is all for today. Write soon.

LOVE, J.B.L.
your little brother

Roby, Texas
Oct 31, 1935
Dear Mildred,

I am writing you after supper, just finished cleaning up supper dishes. I laid out a bunch of stockings and socks to mend after supper, but will finish your letter first. Myrt and Bill left right after dinner. Mrs. Cardwell came up that afternoon and stayed a while with me. Carl plowed in wheat up until Tues. eve., then went to picking cotton. They did the biggest day's picking today *[that]* they've done this year 1,208 lbs. I believe they said. Papa and Carl ran a race and son beat him *[by]* a few lbs. Papa was almost played out when they quit.

I washed Tues. eve. in all of that wind; was afraid to wait for fear it would go to raining, and I could hardly do without washing another week. Marie and Mr. Dean came just a while before I finished washing. She brought me a new oil cloth for the table, but it was too narrow for the table; don't know whether we can exchange it or not. She said Myrt and Bill stayed until after the show Monday night.

How are you feeling tonight? Did you go see a Dr. about your trouble? Maybe it is being on your feet so much causes your kidneys to move so free. Drink lots of water. A glass of warm soda water on going to bed might help you. I know it is a miserable feeling.

Wasn't it warm this eve.? The wind is out of the east tonight; looks like it might shower.

Mildred you surely hid the pecans good. I have never been able to find them; will have to wait until you write me or come back home before I enjoy them.

I will fix your coat for Ella Mae tomorrow; and finished my mending; have some slips to make for Juanita and Ella Mae out of some old skirts.

Puss has taken my pencil away from me so I will have to finish with a pen. Really believe I do better with it anyway, don't you?

Tis is reading Ray's letter and seems to be getting a big kick out of Ray's mistakes. They have already exchanged a few licks; guess it will end in a free-for-all, so don't be surprised at anything *[I]* write.

The fight is on, and I will just quit.

Write real soon and come back to see us when you can.

Lovingly, Mama

Roby, Texas
Nov. 1, 1935
Dear DeDuse,

Gee, you should see how we picked cotton today. I picked two hundred pounds. Dad told me tonight that I sure had a shiny tail, but even if it does I got the cotton. Ha. You see there was a small hole in the seat of my britches; that was what he was telling me about. DeDuse just guess how much we all got today? 1,208 *[pounds]* pretty good for what we had been getting, around 600.

Our school will begin week after next, but don't guess we will get to start; hope so. I don't know *[but]* if we keep picking like we did today, we may.

DeDuse, you know this ink is the messiest stuff you ever saw, but I couldn't find a single pencil. There are scattered all over the place, but don't know where.

DeDuse, I have got Ree's pillowcases done. They are right pretty I think. I hope she thinks so.

DeDuse, Jaber is making fun of my letter. Don't listen to that. I had to think of something.

Well, I'm getting sleepy. So will close.

With love
Ella Mae

Oh, yes, we sure are getting lots of good use out of our yoyos. I am really proud of mine, have broken the string a few times, but it is easy to fix.

P.S. DeDuse, when are you coming home again? My, I sure do look forward for you and Red to come.

This is sure a mix*[ed]* up letter.

Bye Bye

Roby Texas
Nov. 1, 1935
Dear DeDuse,

You ought to *[have]* picked cotton with us today. We picked 1,208 *[pounds]* today, and I picked 178 all day. We are working to get the bale so we won't have to pick much Saturday morning. Puss could pick her sack all day and never get enough to weigh. Tis put down that she finished her pillowcases, but I finished them myself, I finished the hemming. Wednesday evening dad went to the gin, and he told Puss that she had to get 10 pounds. She got 15 and he told her she could come to the house. Mother was gone, and she went to bawling and thought she was down to Miss Cardwell's. She started to go down there, but she came back and Mother was *[illegible]* butter beans and Puss picked me to *[illegible]* pile of cotton if I would let her play with my truck. Well, I guess I had better quit now and go to bed so bye.

Yours truly
Ray Lewis

Oh, yes, Puss picked 45 pounds today and she thought she was doing fine. We play with our yoyos every night. Write real soon.

Roby Texas
Nov 1, 1935
Dear DeDuse

How are you? I am all right and hope you are. In Tis*['s]* letter she said if her tail does shine she got the cotton ha *[illegible]* I picked 157 pounds today.

We have never found another mud-hen on the tank.
THE END
Love, J.B.L

Roby, Tex
Dec. 9, 1935
Dear Mildred,

If I can get my thoughts on paper among the racket of these kiddos, I will get a letter off in tomorrow's mail. Puss is speaking her Xmas piece, Pete is humming, and, well, I just don't know what Jaber is a doing. He has a pile of cotton here on the table that he took out of a stuffed dog. Carl is at Grandma's pulling bolls. Grandma asked him to come and help them out and stay at her house. He thought he could make pretty good money for some things he needed so we let him go for this week and will go for him if it rains.

I guess you and Marie and the rest of them had a big time over the weekend.

Marie has already told you about our new car (new to us). We are real proud of it. We went to Bettie Mae's and Roy's Sunday, Papa, Ella Mae, Juanita and myself. They boys stayed at Clyde's. Grandma and Grandpa were there Sat. night and Sunday. After dinner we drove to Roscoe and seen Dr. Young's new Hospital. It is built of native rock just like his home. It will look real nice when he gets the yard cleaned up. Went on down by the Forrester place, saw old Dutch and Dumie, Jack and Amanda. Everything looked natural except a house for cotton pickers has been built between the house and the barn and near the West fence.

Cliff and Gladys came home with us Sunday eve. Cliff was gathering some bear grass to decorate their windows. He put it in a flowerpot and sticks (beaded candy) on the prongs of grass. It might give you an idea. He said he had several compliments on it.

My pullets have begun to lay real well; got 15 eggs today. We are looking for some baby calves right away, three now by the first of the year. Will sure be glad. Haven't got to kill hogs yet. Hope we do before Xmas.

Papa has all his bundle feed in the stack and *[they]* are

pasturing the fields. Ray and J.B. helped him today. Ray said at supper he thought he would help him go to town tomorrow, but he will go to school. They plowed terraces this evening.

Mildred, I went this eve. to my tomatoes that have covered with weeds and I gathered a gal. of ripe ones. Still some nice green ones left. My paper is giving out.

So Bye Bye
Mama

Roby, Texas
Dec. 10, 1935
Dear DeDuse,

How are you making it at Blackwell? I am making it just fine up here.

Next week is our six-weeks exam. I hope I make passing grades although I have been absent a lot on count of cotton picking. The only test I dread is History. I am afraid I won't make so good on that subject.

DeDuse, I wish you could see our Christmas program. Pete, Jaber and myself are all in a play in our room; Honey *[another nickname for Juanita]* is in some kind of an outfit. Next Thursday night week the 19th of the month is when we are going to have it. The school is going to have their Xmas tree that night. I got a boy's name, Ben Neeper; Pete got a girl's name, Marie Barkley; Jaber got a girl's name, Mary Francis Walker; Honey got a girl's name, Clara Hellen; I don't know her last name. Clara Hellen got Honey's name, too.

DeDuse, I will tell you two things I would very much like to have for Christmas, a package of white drawing paper and a box of crayons. That is what I need for school. I don't care what else I get for Xmas; anything will suit me fine.

Oh! I sure am proud of our car. It sure does ride smooth. You will have to come up and take a ride. Bucky sure is proud of it as well as the rest.

DeDuse, I have me a book to make a report on; the name of it is "Gammy's Wonderful Chair." It seems to be interesting.

Well, have told all the news so will quit.

When are you coming Xmas? Well will see you soon anyway, Bye Bye.
With Love,
Ella Mae.

Blackwell, Tex [likely error instead of Roby]
Dec. 9, 1935
Dear DeDuse,

How are you? I am all right. Me and Jabe stayed out and helped dad haul feed this morning and went and got some post this evening.

When we drawed names this week, I got Marie Barkley's name. I am going to get her a head band.

DeDuse, we went to see Santy Clause the other night, and he gave us all suckers apiece. He was in the courthouse, and we had to go through a hall, and I bet there was a hundred people in there just a pushing and Honey bawled. Ree told us that they would park around the courthouse and we walked around it three times and finally found them a way off on the other street. While we were walking down the street, Jabe got his head hung in a brass horn and walked down the street with his head hung in it, trying to get it out, and Bub like to died laughing. Puss got her head *[illegible]* too

I sure do like our new car. We went to Sweetwater Sunday and stayed all day. I sure did have some fun. Bub gave me a fountain pen; it is a white one; and it is just as good as mine.
With Love
Ray Lewis

Roby, Tex
Dec 9, 1935
Mon night
Dear DeDuse,

How are you? I am all right and hope you are. We have been going to school about a week and Dad said that we would not have to stay out any more.

We have bought us a car, and I like it very much. Sunday we went to Uncle Roy and Bettie Mae. Me and Ray and Boo stayed at Uncle Clyde's.

With Love
your J.B.

Roby, Texas
April 14, 1941
Dear Mildred, Arnold, Bill, Myrt & Billie Nell,

Well, all I have to do is write to you as I have the mumps. I took them in the left side last Monday, and Easter Sunday I had taken in the other side. I guess I will miss nearly two weeks of school.

We have had lots of rain in the last day or two. Sunday morning it rained a big shower and this morning it came another big rain. Ray had just planted sudan *[a grain from a hybrid of sorghum and sudangrass]* so I guess they will get to scratch *[break the crusted topsoil after a rain dries out]* a little.

Me and Mama are going to fix up the smokehouse and get us a hundred chicks for fryers. We were going to fix it his week, but I took the mumps on the other side, and I guess it will be next week before we can fix it. I think Mama and Papa have decided to buy a hundred laying hens instead of fooling with baby chicks.

Ella Mae and Joe did not come in this week, and we did not get a letter from them so we guess they went to Brownwood. Joe had decided to follow up the railroad work, if he could.

I guess you all looked for us Easter, but we looked for you all. We would have come Sat. nite if I hadn't had the mumps. Being as it rained, we looked for you all Sunday night but you didn't come.

Mama is going to send off a biography *[possibly a medical bio]* to Dr. *[illegible]*, and we have to catch the mail man. She is writing to Uncle Cliff and Aunt Gladys, so I told her I would write to you all.

Billie Nell, did you have a big Easter egg hunt? I bet you did. We did not have one because it rained, and we did not have anyone to hide them. Puss tried to get me and Ray to have a hunt with her, but we wouldn't do it.

Well I guess I had better quit as Mama wants to write you a letter.

Love

J.B.

P.S. Come to see us as soon as you can.

Roby, Texas
June 3, 1941
Dear Myrt, Bill, Billie Nell and Mildred & Arnold,

I have been so busy this morning, have just found time to lay down, and I am writing this laying down, hope you can read it or at least the mainest part. Ray has started planting the maize over for the third time; that is what they have in maize on the east side. He bought good seed, and it would not germinate, so he got his seed out of his own crib and treated it and planted it over last week on the west side and has a stand up now on that. The cotton and cane is growing off good. Dad bought his 20 calves last week to put on his Johnson grass & sudan. Yesterday, Papa, Ray, J.B. and I went to Mrs. Rasco's and put up peaches. We put up 46 qt. of plum peaches, canned some for preserves, made some preserves and sweet pickles. We got one-half of these, and we furnished our jars and sugar. He told me yesterday he wanted to give us one bushel of the big yellow plums when they were ripe. The trees were just breaking down with fruit. I hear it thundering round now. Papa has gone to help Mr. Rasco put in a new shaft in his tractor, then he is coming to help Ray get done planting if it don't rain. Jack, Olene, Mrs. Whitworth, Ree & Ralph and us went to the Lake Friday eve., caught fish for supper and fried them there. The men stayed all night, and we came home after supper. They brought fish Sat. morn for all we wanted; took one big one to Johnnie & Ethel, and Ralph took his mother a mess.

Juanita went home with Joe & Ella Mae Sunday eve., and here's the mainest part: We will be at Blackwell Sat. night, both cars if it isn't pouring down rain to go to Coleman Sunday

morning. We will go to the park there for dinner. So Myrt &
Mildred try to manage your chickens so you can go. We want to
leave Blackwell early because we will have to start back early
that eve. Mr. and Mrs. Rasco said they would see after our
chickens & cows.

Ralph thinks he is about to get land measuring job and wants
Ray to help him. Johnnie wants Ray as his helper too if he can't
get Earnest, but Johnnie said he would use J.B.—but I think Dad
is really going to have to use one of them hisself and maybe both
of them if this rain keeps on. Myrt, I believe I promised to mail
your patterns with your slip but have forgot it. Hope I didn't
throw you off about your sewing. Will bring Saturday. Marie
hasn't used it. Birtha Lee Nettleton brought her five new patterns
and Mrs. Crenshaw sent her two. (That was really all she could
use on four dresses)

Hello, Billie Nell. You can get in the car Sunday with us and
go, and she won't have to get out, either mama and daddy can go
to see, Grandma.

Well, I will run look at my beans I'm cooking and call J.B. to
mail this for me.

With Love,
Mama.

CHAPTER ELEVEN

Final Thoughts on the Cotton Culture

Cotton and its accompanying farm culture have long been undervalued for their contributions to Texas and its economy from the very beginning of Anglo settlement until the present day. My folks were minor and virtually unknown players in the waning years of cotton farming before mechanization revolutionized the gathering of the labor-intensive fiber.

While thousands of books have been written on the cattle industry and the Texas cowboy who became an American folk hero, comparatively few have been penned on the cotton farmer in Texas history. With this book I hope to have shone a little light on the lives of one anonymous family who contributed to the industry one tuft at a time through their backbreaking labor. Through their reminiscences I offer a glimpse into the lives of one cotton family from the Roaring Twenties through the Great Depression into World War II. While every family is unique, their experiences are often representative of those of their neighbors, and I hope to have provided some insight into the existence of typical sharecroppers and tenant farmers throughout Texas during those three decades.

While cotton farming may lack the numerous volumes written on the cattle industry, several excellent books on cotton agriculture during the first half of the twentieth century are available for those interested in exploring the topic. If there is a hero in *Cotton-Picking Folks*, it would be Ora Bell Garrett Lewis, the grandmother I never met. She kept the family fed, clothed and together with limited resources. The challenges of Texas farm women like her are documented in *Fertile Ground, Narrow*

Choices: Women on Texas Cotton Farms, 1900-1940, by Rebecca Sharpless. This is an excellent look at the challenges faced by tenant farm wives and their daughters.

A broader look at cotton agriculture during the period is *From Can See to Can't: Texas Cotton Farmers on the Southern Prairies* by Thad Sitton and Dan K. Utley. Another excellent book is *Plains Farmer: The Diary of William G. DeLoach, 1914-1964,* edited by Janet M. Neugebauer. *Plains Farmer* provides an intimate account of an ordinary farmer in an ever-changing world. Both books provide great insight into the daily lives of the cotton farmer.

For a broader look at cotton and its societal and global impact, I recommend Stephen Yafa's *Cotton: The Biography of a Revolutionary Fiber.* The book shows how cotton has shaped history and affected our lives in ways we seldom realize.

I thought it important in this volume to include summaries, both in my introduction and in their own words, of the ensuing lives of the Lewis siblings once they left the farm. The one enduring theme in all of their recollections was the love of family. The one topic I did remove for the most part from the family memoirs in this volume was the specifics of Ray's and John's World War II experiences. I have opted instead to publish them in a future volume. My greatest hope is that this volume is a fitting testament to the spirit and sacrifice of all those anonymous families of all races who worked the cotton fields in the first half of the twentieth century.

Mildred, Ray, Ella Mae, Marie, John, Myrt and
Juanita at Lewis Family Reunion, circa 1990

Acknowledgements

A book never comes about without the help of many others. In this case, I owe my father and his siblings my enduring gratitude for taking the time to document their lives growing up on a tenant farm during the Great Depression. Without their time and devotion, this project would have never been possible. So thank you Dad, Mildred, Marie, Myrt, Ella Mae, Ray and Juanita.

As the family historian, I've been blessed to receive numerous documents and photographs for my files. I owe an especial thanks to my brother Marc and his wife Lee Ann for running down some additional photos for this project. I should also thank my surviving cousins Billie Nell, Reatha, Charlotte, Karyl, Carl, Jerry, Harvey, Gary and Mike for all the good times we had growing up. Not to be forgotten are our late cousins Larry, Vicki and Wayland whose lives are remembered fondly by all of us.

The striking cover photo was colorized by an extraordinary photographer, Jim Bean of San Angelo. Thanks, Jim, for the time and talent you invested in this project.

Also, I must thank Douglas Bagley for working Mom's and Dad's place in their declining years and for reviewing on multiple occasions the opening chapter of this book.

As this is a book about the family that shaped my young life, I should thank my family, starting with wife Harriet for her enduring love and support. We were blessed to have son Scott and daughter Melissa. They brought into the family their spouses Celeste and John, who are fine Christian parents and role models for our grandchildren. Hannah, Cora, Miriam, Carys and Jackson (I call them *The Grands*) have been sources of great joy for Harriet and me. All that is missing is our late grandson Benjamin, whose memory remains with us in spirit.

Finally, I should thank the publisher of Bariso Press for taking on this project and making my family's memoirs available for posterity.

Author Biography

PRESTON LEWIS is the award-winning author of 44 works of fiction and nonfiction, including *Cat Tales of the Old West: Poems, Puns & Perspectives on Frontier Felines*. His article "Bluster's Last Stand" published in *True West* earned him the first of his two Spur Awards from Western Writers of America (WWA). His second Spur came for *Blood of Texas*, his sweeping historical novel on the Texas Revolution.

His other fiction works have garnered four Will Rogers Gold Medallion Awards, two for written western humor and two for short stories. Five of the seven novels in his comic western series *The Memoirs of H.H. Lomax* have received various national writing honors.

In 2021 Lewis was inducted into the Texas Institute of Letters for his literary accomplishments. He is a past president of WWA and the West Texas Historical Association, which has honored him three times with Elmer Kelton Awards for best creative work on West Texas.

Lewis holds a bachelor's degree from Baylor University and a master's degree from Ohio State University, both in journalism. Additionally, he has a second master's degree in history from Angelo State University. He began his professional career working for four Texas newspapers and then moving into higher education communications/marketing at Texas Tech University and Angelo State University, where he retired.

Lewis lives in San Angelo, Texas, with wife Harriet.

E-mail: prestonlewisauthor@gmail.com
Facebook: prestonlewisauthor
Website: prestonlewisauthor.com

Made in the USA
Columbia, SC
01 August 2022